Make Your Own FUN

Josie Curran lives in Devon with her boyfriend Barney, two children Herbie and Kitty, and Otter the dog. When she's not coming up with new and marvellous ways to fill your time, she works at the children's charity Kids Company.

www.josie-curran.com

Make Your Own Fun

Josie Curran

Illustrated by Alice Stevenson

MACMILLAN CHILDREN'S BOOKS

First published 2009 by Boxtree
an imprint of Pan Macmillan

This edition published 2012 by Macmillan Children's Books
a division of Macmillan Publishers Limited
20 New Wharf Road, London N1 9RR
Basingstoke and Oxford
Associated companies throughout the world
www.panmacmillan.com

ISBN 978-0-330-54468-9

1 3 5 7 9 8 6 4 2

A CIP catalogue record for this book is available from
the British Library.

Printed and bound by CPI Group (UK) Ltd, Croydon CR0 4YY

Contents

Dedicated to our son Herbie Hunter Girling
and all the fun he has ahead of him

Introduction

Once upon a time, before television and computers, playing games came naturally to kids. After-school hours, weekends and holidays used to be packed with homespun fun – adventures in secret dens and hideaways, re-enactments of famous battles and journeys to magical mystical worlds.

As children, my siblings and I were masters of make-your-own fun. From the glimmer of dawn to the deepening of dusk, we could be found playing outside or up in the attic, lost in worlds of our own imagining. From sailing cardboard boxes across the lawn to imaginary husky-racing down the lane, we were able to create our own entertainment – a skill that meant our parents could take us anywhere and be assured that we'd soon disappear off and start having more fun than them.

Kids have an innate ability to entertain themselves and, with a spot of guidance and encouragement, can squirrel themselves away and play for hours. I'm not saying that TV and computer games are the devil's incarnation (believe me, I'm more than aware of the saving grace that five minutes in front of the TV can provide), but there are some fundamental skills to be learnt as well as a far deeper pleasure to be gained when a child creates their own entertainment.

The way children play has changed dramatically over the past twenty years. When we were kids, we had the freedom to run around and play as we pleased. I was lucky enough to grow up in an era when we were able to help the postman with his early-morning rounds and play in the streets until the long shadows turned to dusk. Sadly, due to increased fears around child safety, most kids these days are denied this freedom and the life-affirming pleasure of playing and learning in the great outdoors. As television and computer games provide ever-ready distractions that also keep kids well within sight and earshot, nature's playground and children's innate ability to muster fun out of thin air are becoming less familiar concepts than ever before.

It is widely agreed that play helps kids to understand the world and their place in it, and I believe that children should be encouraged to create their own fun. Play gives children an opportunity to learn to socialise and resolve conflicts, and it also helps them to develop their imagination and creativity. By showing your young charges how to make their own fun, you'll be preparing them for life's triumphs and tribulations – as well as buying yourself some well-earned peace.

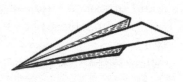

About This Book

This book is designed to ensure childhood boredom is banished at home along with the TV. A lot of the games are great for grown-ups to play, too; before you realise it, you could find yourself getting stuck in as well.

The book has been structured in such a way that wherever you are and whatever the weather, you should be able to find your way to some inspiring ideas for fun. It also includes appropriate warnings throughout, and some of the games and activities do require parental support. In the interests of health and safety, I am obliged to suggest that you exercise common sense and parental caution.

The purpose of this book is to help kids make their own fun, but it will also provide a helping hand to anyone who spends time with kids. It's packed full of ideas and inspiration to get kids creating and crafting, playing and no doubt bickering – but at least they'll be creating the fun themselves. I hope the book sets you on the path to creating some magical memories for your kids to share.

One
The
Great Outdoors

Thinking back to our childhoods, many of us remember a magical time of freedom and discovery, indulging in the pleasures of nature's playground. Sunny days saw kids playing out from dawn through to the hazy shadows of dusk; long bike rides led to secret hideaways and pools of water bubbling with frogspawn. Pond dipping and newspaper kites, scavenger hunts and mud pies all recall a time of innocence when the great outdoors was the only chosen place to play.

If you're keen to ensure your child develops similar happy memories of their own, give them an encouraging shove out of the back door. With a helping hand they'll soon discover the wealth of delights on offer and you'll be struggling to coax them back in.

The following chapter is brimming with ideas for encouraging your kids to get outside and stuck into enjoying the world beyond your window. From sunny springtime pursuits to frosty winter frolics, there should be something here to captivate kids whatever the weather's doing outside.

Forest Fancy Dress

What's the game?

Kids have the imagination to see another world where others only see ordinary things. A tree becomes an old man or a bush a bumbling warthog. You can encourage the exploration of this parallel universe by instigating a game of fancy dress using the trimmings of nature. Think tree soldiers decked out in leaf armour and stick swords or a forest queen with a fern-frond crown and a cloak of golden corn and you'll get the general idea. You need to keep an eye on their foraging to ensure their enthusiasm doesn't lead them to rustle up something out of nature's more interesting finds. I know of a child who fashioned a hat out of a dried cowpat, while my younger sister was particularly keen on her dead-adder necklace. Pretty creative stuff, but it might make you feel a little nervous.

This game's best played at the height of summer or when autumn brings its rich and deep tones to your fancy-dress pickings. It's also a brilliant way to keep your kids entertained if you're doing some pruning. Your cutting cast-offs could inspire the look of the season.

What do I need to play it?

Half the fun of this game is in getting your gang to forage for fashion finds. Encourage them to form an idea of their 'look' as soon as they start to gather material so that they can pick items that add to their outfit. Ideas and inspirations on what they might use are included below.

As they'll need a little help in pulling their outfits together, I'd also suggest bringing the following with you:

- A stapler with lots of staples (vital)
- Card (flexible enough so it can be bent to form the shape of a hat or waistband)

- Scissors
- Old pieces of material and clothes – old sheets or even an old cotton dress, top or shorts are perfect
- Some strong glue – I'd test it out beforehand. You need something strong enough to bond leaves, etc., to paper
- Double-sided tape
- String
- Some rugs with old newspaper spread on top as protection, or some plastic sheeting if you have it
- A knitting needle

How many kids and what age?

This activity is brilliant for large or small groups and works for all ages, as long as an adult is around to provide a helping hand.

How do I play it?

- Once the kids have collected together their finds, you need to get them set up somewhere where they can be creative. Put some rugs down on the ground if it's dry, or plastic sheets if you have them, lay out your make-and-do supplies and get them started. Below are some ideas designed to provide some inspiration.
  - A queen's cloak: every forest queen needs a cloak to ensure the masses are aware of her majestic status. Get an old length of material and cut a strip of card that can be fixed at the top to create the collar. Gather together a collection of items with height (corn, bracken or even long grass are all perfect) and get your kids to lay these out on the strip of card. Fix them in place before finally attaching the card to the material as a majestic collar. Leaves or other garden finds can then be stuck all over the material.

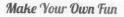

- A king's crown: no forest royal is properly dressed without their regal crown. Take a strip of card and curve it around the child's head, ensuring there is enough overlapping length to staple it together when made. Next, get the kids to fix their leafy jewels to the crown using a stapler, or stick them down using double-sided tape.

- A hula girl: Hawaiian hula girls are adept at using nature's delights to create their dancing outfits. You can create a similar but non-tropical look using garden or woodland finds such as grasses or bracken. To create a hula necklace, tie a long length of string to a knitting needle, ensuring there is a large knot at one end, and get the kids to thread a pile of leaves (or flowers if you can spare them) onto the string to create the necklace. Tie up the two ends once done.

  To create a hula skirt, cut a strip of card and measure it on the child's waist, ensuring there is some extra overlapping to fix at the end. Next, using either double-sided tape or a stapler, get the child to fix long lengths of corn, grass, bracken or whatever they've managed to gather onto the card. You'll need to ensure their finds aren't too heavy for the weight of your card.

- Safety note: if you're using a stapler to fix everything in place, it's probably best to get the child to lay out everything as they'd like it to be arranged and then an adult can come along and do the stapling at the end.

Broom Polo

What's the game?

As a horse-loving, city-living kid, I spent much of my childhood cycling around car parks on my trusty rusty bike, imagining it was a noble chestnut steed galloping through the countryside. After coming across the game of Polo in one of my well-worn pony books, my bike–horse game was soon adapted to include our kitchen broom and I persuaded my younger sisters to join me in a game of Broom Polo.

This game is great fun to play with a gaggle of kids who are adept on bikes and looking for some alternative entertainment.

What do I need to play it?

One ball, and a bike and a broom per player, with tin cans for goalposts.

How many kids and what age?

You can play it with two kids, but two teams of four (as in a real game of Polo) is the ideal scenario. Kids really need to be aged eight and upwards.

How do I play it?

- If there are more than two kids, get them into teams.
- Each player mounts their bike and grasps the broom as if it were a polo mallet, with the sweeping end primed to hit the ball.
- Each 'chukka' (period of play) lasts seven minutes and you can choose to play between four and seven chukkas, depending on how much time you've got.
- The object of the game is to score goals. Hitting the ball across the line with your broom scores a goal. If a ball is knocked across the line by your bike rather than your broom, this is also counted as a goal.
- The team with the most goals at the end of the chukkas wins.

Torch Tag

What's the game?

Torch Tag is a brilliant game to play with kids in the garden at night. It's a handy way to help those who are scared of the dark overcome their fears as it changes the dangerous darkness into a playground of fun. You need to make sure you set clear parameters of play to prevent intrepid children foraging too far off in search of their favoured hiding place.

What do I need to play it?

A strong torch and an enclosed area to play.

How many kids and what age?

You need at least three kids to make the game work and they should really be aged five and over.

How do I play it?

- Decide who's going to be 'it' first. All the other kids spread out and hide. If you're playing with particularly young kids, an adult should go and hide with them.

- Whoever's 'it' counts to twenty (or more if you're playing in a larger area) and then shouts, 'Coming, ready or not.' They must then hunt around for the others, using their torch. If they manage to catch anyone in their beam, that child is out. The last child to be caught is 'it' on the next go.

- Safety note: try to avoid playing in an area with a pond or river or similar area of risk. You need to be certain that your gang know the area they're playing in well enough to prevent them getting into danger, particularly when scrabbling around in the dark.

Emily's Foraging Game

What's the game?

This is my dear friend Emily's favourite game. It involves sending your kids out into the forest, garden or patio to race to find all the nature items on your list. Depending on where you are, you can theme it in all sorts of ways.

This game's a particularly brilliant way to persuade reluctant young walkers that there's more to a country walk than dragging your feet.

What do I need to play it?

A pen and a piece of paper for each team.

How many kids and what age?

Great for all ages and for large or small groups.

How do I play it?

- Players choose to play individually or in teams. If you're playing with very young kids, it's best to pair them with an adult.

- Each team is given an identical list of natural finds or other landmarks that they're likely to come across on their walk. For example, you might choose to put an oak leaf or a lichen-covered twig on your list. Alternatively, depending on the location of your walk, you might opt for a more urban-themed list, or even ask kids to take cameraphone pictures of road signs or markings spotted along the way.

- The first team back with a completed list wins.

- An extra level of competition can be added by scoring items depending on how difficult they are to find.

Bow Selecta!

What's the game?

There's a Robin Hoodesque appeal to the idea of crafting a bow and arrow from woodland finds before leaping from log to tree in battle. Your kids should find it lots of fun to play.

This is a great way to encourage reluctant walkers to join you on a country stomp. By recreating a world where they can rob the rich to feed the poor, you'll find yourself battling to keep up with their pace. Just make sure you warn them that firing at random walkers is out of bounds.

What do I need to play it?

You'll need some flexible branches for the bows, and some dry sticks that have been on the ground for a long time for the arrows. You'll also need some string and a sharp knife.

How many kids and what age?

Ideal to play with a couple of kids aged seven and upwards.

How do I play it?

- First of all, get your kids to pick their bow branches, making sure they're flexible enough to create a good twang. They need to be about a metre in length.

- Next, select some sticks for the arrows. These can be collected from the ground, as the drier they are the better. They need to be about thirty to forty centimetres long and fairly straight.

- The grown-up should then cut some small indentations about five centimetres down from each end of the bow to hold the string in place. Then tie a long piece of string tightly in place at the top and fasten it at the other end so that it creates a bow-like shape. The string should be taut enough to twang.

- Finally, the grown-up should take each of the arrow sticks and splice them to create a pointy end. You need to be careful just how pointy you make them, because if they are too sharp and get misfired, there could be a nasty accident.

- Once prepared, it's really important that you give your kids a lesson on how to use their newly crafted bow and arrow, placing particular emphasis on the fact that they should only fire them in a direction that is clear of anyone else.

Den Days

What's the game?

Making a den is an essential part of any child's world. Equally, finding half your kitchen cupboard or linen closet rotting in the undergrowth is a fundamental parenting experience. Dens indulge a child's creative desire to build and make a home of their own. If crafted well, your child's den could see them squirrelled away for most of the summer, affording you time to indulge your own idea of summer fun.

What do I need to play it?

You need a safe place to play and access to den-making material such as logs and sticks, as well as something to pad out the roof. It's also good to have some strong string to hand to bind things together and, if an adult is there to help, it's useful to bring a sledgehammer to bang thick sticks or stakes into the ground. If you're not so worried about achieving a natural look, then a plastic sheet to cover the ground is pretty useful to ensure your kids don't roll in looking like Stig of the Dump every day.

How many kids and what age?

This is best played with small groups of kids aged five and upwards.

How do I play it?

- First of all, you need to find your den location. This might take some time and cause some intense debate. You need to ensure your vegetable patch doesn't become colonised and that building doesn't take place on your bed of spring bulbs.

- Once you've found a location, you then need to discuss and agree on what design your den is going to take. If you've found somewhere in the undergrowth with a natural room, it's all about starting to build your den from the inside out. This means crawling in and starting to create walls using sticks banged into the ground and weaving other sticks in and out as padding. You might want to stretch plastic sheeting across the roof and over the ground at this point, or if you're going for a natural look then creating padding from dried leaves, bracken, corn or grass is another great option.

- If you're building your den out in the open, you need to create your structure from scratch. One way to do this is to create a triangular tent-like structure:

  1. Bang two strong sticks or logs into the ground so that they lean together to create a triangle (you might need to chisel a point at one end to get them to go into the ground). Now bind these together using string or strips of bark.

  2. Next, take your longest log and rest it on the apex of the other two logs, with the other end trailing down to the ground. This provides your basic tent structure.

  3. Create the walls by leaning other logs up against the long one and then weaving flexible branches in and out of them to create the wall.

  4. Finally, to add extra padding, collect together leaves, corn, bracken or old branches and weave these in and out of your log structure to create a padded roof.

- Safety note: if the den isn't in your garden, you need to ensure there's an adult nearby to keep an eye on the kids.

- You can also get your kids to create a magical hideaway in the comfort of your own home using chairs and sheets: see Hideaway Castles in 'When You're Stuck Indoors'.

Cola Volcano

What's the activity?

If your kids are fans of exploding messes, this one will be a winner. I've included it in the outdoor chapter of this book, as the mess the experiment creates is best made outside.

What do I need?

For this activity you need a full two-litre bottle of cola, a packet of Mentos mints (I haven't been able to make it work with any other type of mint), some paper and a playing card.

How many kids and what age?

This one will delight kids of all ages and is great for small groups.

What do we do?

- First of all, take the lid off the bottle and place the playing card over the top. Next, create a tube of paper and position this on the card above the bottle, then drop five Mentos down the tube.

- When you're ready, slide the card out from under the tube so that the mints drop into the bottle and step back to avoid the exploding volcano.

- If you're looking for a more dramatic effect, add more mints.

Home-Made Volcano

What's the activity?

This is a great way to fill an afternoon and end it with a big bang. It's similar to the Cola Volcano, but this version encourages kids to be a bit more creative and draws on the contents of your kitchen cupboard. In this activity, the object is to create a volcano that explodes at the end in a big, red, fizzing, foaming . . . erm . . . mess. This is why kids love it so much.

What do I need?

Some air-drying clay, some suitable paint that can be used on the clay once it's dry (you need volcanic colours, so brown, black, yellow, orange and red are ideal), an old shampoo bottle, a board on which to build the volcano, some bicarbonate of soda, some vinegar (regular malt is ideal) and some red food colouring.

How many kids and what age?

Great for kids of all ages and all group sizes.

What do we do?

- Cut the top off your shampoo bottle and attach the base to the centre of the board using a piece of clay.
- Next, use the clay to build a volcano around the shampoo bottle.
- Once the clay has dried, get the kids painting the volcano with the browns at the bottom building up to the blacks, reds and yellows as you get closer to the hot top.
- Leave this to dry for a bit. In the meantime, concoct your exploding volcano mixture by mixing together a tablespoon of bicarbonate of soda with three or four drops of food colouring and scrape this mixture into the top of the volcano so it falls to the bottom of the shampoo bottle.
- When you're ready, carefully pour in a quarter of a teacup of malt vinegar, step back and watch the explosion.

Pooh Sticks

What's the game?

Pooh Sticks were a much-anticipated feature of my childhood holidays in Devon. There was a small stone bridge over the river in the bottom field that we used to hang over to play. We spent hours assessing the water to work out where it flowed fastest, nudging each other along to get to the prized spot as we steeled ourselves for the off.

Pooh Sticks originated from A. A. Milne's tales of Winnie-the-Pooh. The game is described in *The House at Pooh Corner* when Christopher Robin and Pooh play on a bridge, throwing fir cones in the water.

Ever since the publication of Milne's book in the 1920s, the endearing magic of the game has ensured it is passed on from generation to generation. Its popularity is such that since 1984 a World Pooh Sticks Championship is held at Day's Lock in Oxfordshire each year.

What do I need to play it?

A stream or river with a bridge, and some sticks or similar items that you might find lying around.

How many kids and what age?

As many as will fit on your bridge. Great for all ages, though make sure an adult is holding any young kids tightly as they chuck their sticks over the top.

How do I play it?

- Players hunt out their chosen stick and memorise what it looks like.

- Next, players must all position themselves along the side of the bridge with the water flowing towards them.

- On the word 'Go!', players all drop their sticks into the water, then turn and race to the other side to see whose gets there first.

Wally

What's the game?

Any boy who's spent time at an English secondary school should recognise this game. Its simplicity and capacity to include big groups of kids have made it a favourite in school playgrounds across the country for years.

What do I need to play it?

A football or tennis ball and a wall to kick it off.

How many kids and what age?

You can start off small, but it works brilliantly for groups of all sizes. As long as a child can kick a ball they'll pick it up fairly quickly.

How do I play it?

- If you're using a tennis ball, you can play with your hands or even a tennis racket. If you're playing with a football, use your feet.

- Choose a wall that's at least two metres high.

- The first player hits or kicks the ball towards the wall, ensuring that it bounces once before hitting the wall. As the ball bounces back off the wall, it must then bounce once on the ground before the next player hits or kicks the ball back.

- A player is out if they fail to hit the ball, if they don't make the ball bounce before hitting the wall, or if they miss the wall entirely. The winner is the last person left in.

Stone Skimming

What's the game?

Stone Skimming evokes images of father and son silhouetted against the sunset as they skim their stones into the water from the beach. Its nostalgic appeal ensures it is passed on down the line, guaranteeing it a long and healthy future.

My dad taught us the art of skimming while on a family holiday on Islay, a small island in the Scottish Outer Hebrides. It used to infuriate us girls that the boys seemed to have an innate ability to master the flicking motion and to judge the impetus required to bounce a smooth flat pebble across the water. Stone Skimming is an art that is attained through practice.

What do I need to play it?

A collection of small flat pebbles and a stretch of water.

How many kids and what age?

Perfect to play solo or with however many you like. Kids can learn the art from five upwards.

How do I play it?

- Carefully select a collection of small, flat pebbles. Everyone has a different view on which shape works best, but I've always found the rounder and flatter the better.

- Stand on the shore or bank and use a flicking motion with your hand to make your pebble bounce across the water.

- The winner is the person whose pebble achieves the most bounces before it sinks.

- An alternative version is to skim stones across a river so that they land (ideally) in the same spot on the other side. We often play this from our houseboat and have just about mastered the degree of flick required to skim the stone so that it hits the bench on the opposite bank – obviously we only attempt this when it's free of dozing grannies.

Bicycle Obstacle Course

What's the game?

This offers an advanced lesson in cycling proficiency by getting your young friends to cycle their way around a designated course.

What do I need to play it?

A child's bike and whatever you have to hand to create an obstacle course.

How many kids and what age?

As many as would like to play. They need to be of bike-riding age and have mastered cycling without stabilisers.

How do I play it?

- First you need to create your course, using objects from around your house or garden. Think about flowerpots they could weave in and out of, a bridge made from a plank across your garden pond (if you're feeling brave), a basket hung from a tree that they need to grab as they cycle past, or a challenging track to cycle over, made, for example, from an old duvet laid on the grass. The options are endless. Your best bet is to have a dig around the paraphernalia in your garden shed or attic.

- Once the basic course is completed, challenge each child to cycle around the course, completing allocated tasks on the way.

Frozen T-Shirt Competition

What's the game?

Definitely one for the summer. This game involves racing to be the first to put on a frozen T-shirt.

What do I need to play it?

A T-shirt for every player and a freezer to prepare them in.

How many kids and what age?

As many as you like.

How do I play it?

- T-shirts are thoroughly soaked the day before and either screwed up and tied into a tight ball or folded up as if to be put away. They are then placed in the freezer overnight. The more water left in the T-shirt the harder it is to put on, so it's up to you whether you want to wring it out or not.

- Players line up with the frozen T-shirts on the floor in front of them. On the signal, players race to put their T-shirts on.

- The first to get their T-shirt all the way on wins.

Slip and Slide

What's the game?

When I was a child, summers used to be as they should be –
full of sunshine and blissfully hot. I can remember endless
after-school hours or balmy weekends playing on our
waterslide. It was the perfect way to prevent a gathering of
hot kids turning crotchety.

What do I need to play it?

A long grass area, ideally on a slope, a hose attached to a tap
and a long sheet of plastic.

How many kids and what age?

How ever many are around to play. Great for kids of all ages.

How do I play it?

- Lay out the plastic sheet on the grass. Turn the hose on
  and let the water run down the sheet from one end. Kids
  then charge towards and skid down the plastic, getting
  soaked and squealing along the way.

Two

When You're
Stuck Indoors

A rain-sodden Saturday or wet half-term can present one of the greatest parenting challenges. It can be a battle of wills to come up with a new and engaging idea for fun, rather than admitting defeat and heaving a sigh of resignation as the familiar beep-beep sounds of the computer-game console resume. The following chapter will give you enough ideas for a year's worth of indoor fun and frolics that will have you constantly dazzling and amazing your kids.

Mrs Beskin's Brilliant Ball-Bashing Game

What's the game?

This is a great game to wear out your kids and allow them to let off some steam when stuck inside on a rainy day. You'll need to have enough room to swing a cat (well, swish a newspaper in this case) as it does involve some leaping about, so some furniture manoeuvring is probably in order.

What do I need to play it?

A stopwatch, a pile of old newspapers and a blindfold per player.

How many kids and what age?

A minimum of four kids aged six and upwards.

How do I play it?

- Get the kids to prepare a pile of at least twenty scrunched-up balls of newspaper and lay out some clothes or a piece of rope to mark out the two sides of the pitch.

- Next, split the kids into two teams and position them on either side of the rope with half the paper balls on either side.

- The object of the game is to get rid of as many of the newspaper balls on your side of the pitch as possible within a minute, with both teams throwing the balls over to their opponents' side. Teams can decide if players should only throw the balls one at a time or simultaneously.

- At the end of the minute, the team with the fewest balls on their side scores a point. The game plays on until one of the teams reaches five points and they're declared the winner.

The Impossible Egg

What's the activity?

This should befuddle your kids and get them pondering the marvels of science. It's a bit like the eternal question of how those ships end up in glass bottles: how do you get an egg inside one?

What do I need?

A glass bottle, a peeled boiled egg and some matches.

How many kids and what age?

Great for small groups of kids of all ages.

What do we do?

- First get the kids to peel the boiled egg so that it's completely shell-free.

- Next, light about four or five matches over the bottle and drop them all in before getting one of the kids to quickly put the boiled egg over the mouth of the bottle.

- The heated air inside the bottle will expand and take up more room. When the warm air cools down it creates a lower pressure inside the bottle than outside, and the egg will be sucked inside.

Ringing Hide and Seek

What's the game?

This one's a modern twist on Hide and Seek in which clues are transmitted by mobile-phone calls.

What do I need to play it?

Two mobile phones.

How many kids and what age?

A minimum of three kids aged seven and upwards.

How do I play it?

- Whoever's hiding first takes one mobile phone and hides, while the others count to sixty before shouting, 'Coming, ready or not!'

- The seekers take the other mobile phone and proceed to hunt around the house to try to find the hidden person. If they can't find them after sixty seconds, they can call the mobile phone and the hider must give one clue to his or her whereabouts.

- While one child is making the call, the other children need to run around the house listening to the ringing of the mobile phone, as this will also provide a clue as to where the child is hidden.

- A maximum of three clues can be given and then, if the hider is still not to be found, they are declared the winner.

Blindfold Taste Challenge

What's the game?

My friend Zoe plays this game with her young cousins whenever she goes to stay with them. It's a brilliant way to encourage kids to engage with their senses, challenging them to learn to use their noses.

What do I need to play it?

A selection of smelly foods, some small dishes to put them in, a pen and paper.

How many kids and what age?

Great for a small gang or a huge party. Works for kids of all ages, though the younger ones might need a hand to write down what they can smell.

How do I play it?

- Choose a selection of smelly foods (between six and eight is ideal) and put these in your small dishes. Parmesan cheese, vinegar, chopped-up ginger and pieces of orange are all good options.

- Arrange the dishes on the kitchen table and get the kids blindfolded in the other room. Once they're ready, lead them in one by one and ask them to smell each dish in turn. When finished, lead them back to the other room, where they take off their blindfolds and write down what they think they were asked to smell.

- Once everyone has made their guesses, reveal what each dish was, giving a point for each correct guess. The child with the most points wins.

Indoor Rainbows

What's the activity?

I spent years chasing rainbows when I was a child. It wasn't that I believed there was a pot of gold waiting at the end; it was the prospect of reaching in and feeling the colours. Sadly such daydreams were destroyed by the reality of physics, but this little experiment should hopefully keep the magic alive for your charges.

What do I need?

A sunny day, some plain white paper, a mirror, a large glass full of water and a table near a window.

How many kids and what age?

Great for small groups of all ages.

What do we do?

- Fill the glass with water and carefully position it so that a small part of the glass is balancing on the edge of the table so the sun can shine through it onto the floor.

- Next, position a piece of paper on the floor so that the sunlight reflects through the glass of water and a rainbow forms on the paper.

- If you're worried about balancing a glass on the edge of a table, the same experiment can be done using a saucepan and a mirror. With this approach, you need to reflect the sunlight off the water in the pan, onto the mirror and then onto the paper. It takes a bit of fiddling about but is worth the effort.

Blow Football

What's the game?

Blow football is the sort of game that could absorb and amuse your kids for an entire wet week stuck inside. It requires you to have a modicum of patience, because if the game is to be played properly your table needs to be taped up in pieces of cardboard. To achieve an even playing field, kids should ideally be of roughly the same height and lung capacity, as their success depends on how far they can lean across the table and how hard they can blow the ball.

What do I need to play it?

Ideally a decent-sized table to play on, but if this proves difficult you can build your pitch on the carpet. For table play you need lots of strips of cardboard about ten centimetres in height, enough to go all the way around the table, and some tape to fix them in place that won't damage the woodwork. If you're playing on the carpet, the simplest set-up is to use T-shirts rolled up in long lengths to create the pitch barriers. You also need a straw for each player and a ping-pong ball.

How many kids and what age?

Ideally played with two opposing players or two teams of kids aged eight and upwards.

Make Your Own Fun

How do I play it?

- First of all, set up the pitch by either taping the cardboard strips to the sides of the table or laying out lines of T-shirts on the floor to create the barriers. You need to leave goal-sized holes at each end for the ping-pong ball to satisfyingly fly through when a goal is triumphantly scored.

- Next, place the ball in the middle of the table with the two teams stood at either end.

- The aim of the game is to score goals by blowing the ping-pong ball through the opponent's goal. Players must not move from behind their end of the table, and it's also against the rules to use their hands or touch the ball with their straw or face. All scoring and defending must be achieved with the players' own blowing power.

- N.B. If you're playing on a particularly long table, you might want to agree that players are allowed to move a little further up the sides of the table. Use a chair or something similar to mark the maximum distance they can move along.

- One point is awarded for each goal scored. After a goal, the ball is placed back in the centre of the table and on the word 'Go!' play should recommence.

- If the ball is blown off the pitch, it should be placed back on at the point at which it went off – pretty much like in a real game of football.

- Play continues for the length of the pre-agreed time period and the player (or players if you're playing in teams) with the most goals at the end is declared the winner.

Hideaway Castles

What's the game?

A magical way to while away a day stuck inside is to get your kids to create a secret hideaway castle. You can get all creative if you decide to help the kids out, but half the fun for them is to create a secret world of their own where grown-ups aren't allowed. Supply them with the props and some advice, then leave them to get stuck in.

What do I need to play it?

Have a rummage through your linen cupboards and up in the loft to see what you can dig out. Large rugs and sheets are good for creating canopy-like shapes. You may want to indulge the kids by allowing them to decorate their castle with Christmas decorations. To dress up the little kings and queens, cut paper crowns out of card and dig out old dressing gowns to create regal cloaks.

How many kids and what age?

Ideal for kids aged three to six. It works perfectly for little groups.

Make Your Own Fun

How do I play it?

- Give your kids a helping hand in choosing the best place to build their castle and equip them with draping equipment to inspire their imaginations. You need somewhere with tall furniture that can be safely and securely pushed and pulled around to create the walls of the structure. A great way to do it is to pull one corner of a sofa away from the wall to make a triangle shape, then create a roof with a sheet supported by chairs. Alternatively, position four dining chairs in a square and use sheets and rugs as canopies, though this does have the risk of collapsing in on the kids if things get boisterous inside. It all depends on where you're happy for the kids to play.

- Once the structure is in place, you might want to allow them to decorate their castle by giving them a rug and cushions to use inside and even provide them with some Christmas decorations that you can safety-pin to the sheets.

- Finally, get them kitted out in their regal wear by giving them some card cut into crown shapes for them to decorate before gluing together and positioning on their heads. You can also create a royal cloak out of an old dressing gown or coat and help them make a royal sceptre using a tin-foil ball attached to a broom handle.

- Once set up, this should keep them busy for the rest of the day. You could even serve their royal lunch and supper inside their den if you're feeling brave. The longer the magical royal world is indulged, the more time you'll have to yourself.

Oxford and Cambridge Boat Race

What's the game?

This is a trick in the guise of a game. I once played it on an ageing aunt and ended up with an old lady in near-apoplectic shock. It requires friends and family who can take a joke, but kids seem to love to play it again and again and again, yep, and again.

What do I need to play it?

A straw and a cork for each player. A fairly shallow container to make a 'lake' out of (a roasting tray is perfect) and a table to put it on.

How many kids and what age?

Ideally played with two to four kids aged six and over.

How do I play it?

- Fill your lake with water and get your boats lined up at the start.

- The nominal aim of the game is for players to race their boats across the lake by blowing them through a straw.

- Get the players hyped up and poised to start blowing. Then, just at the point when their faces are closest to the water, the host slams the table really hard as they shout 'Go!' so that all the water splashes up and soaks them.

Make Your Own Fun

Banker Broker

What's the game?

This is a game that used to be played by kids living in Brooklyn, New York. It's a brilliant bit of portable entertainment that can be rolled out wherever you are.

What do I need to play it?

A bowl and some nuts if you want to follow the traditional rules, but coppers, marbles or even stones work just as well. You need about ten nuts or coins per child.

How many kids and what age?

A good three or four and they need to be old enough to have a basic grasp of maths.

How do I play it?

- Choose who's going to be banker, leaving the rest of the players to be depositors.
- The banker places the bowl on the ground and draws a line half a metre or so away.
- Depositors pay the banker one nut to play, and then in turn throw the remaining nine nuts to try to get as many as possible into the bowl.
- If an even number of items land in the bowl, the banker pays out, returning the nuts that landed in the bowl and matching them from the bank. If an odd number lands in the bowl, the depositor loses them all.
- If a depositor manages to get all their nuts in the bowl, they become the banker.

Marbles

What's the game?

There was a huge marbles fad when I was at school, serviced by a brilliant toyshop stocked with the most deliciously impressive selection. I can remember scraping and saving until I had enough to warrant a trip to the shops and would drive my mum to distraction as I pored over the marbles on offer. There were Oilies and Cat's Eyes, Steelies and Onion Skins, or the colourful but common Toothpaste ones – the best choice if you were playing for 'keeps'.

This is another great game to have stashed in your bag and at the ready when the melodious whines of 'I'm bored' start to kick in.

What do I need to play it?

A selection of marbles and somewhere to play. You need a minimum of five marbles per player. Ideally, you should try to sort the marbles so that each player's are distinctly different to prevent potential mix-ups and tears. You can play on any hard surface, but you need to be able to mark out the area of play – chalk on tarmac is particularly good for this. We used to play on drain covers at school and use the different indentations to mean different things.

How many kids and what age?

This game is best played in twos, but if you've got a large group and enough marbles, you can run a tournament-style event in which the winners of each heat go on to play the ultimate endgame. Kids really need to be six and upwards to properly grasp the rules.

How do I play it?

- Get the kids into pairs and issue each one with their five marbles: four for playing with and one for shooting with. Try to get the sets of four to be as distinctly different as possible so the kids can remember whose is whose.

- Mark out the area of play. Ideally the space should be a circle half a metre in diameter.

- Players then place their four playing marbles anywhere in the designated area of play and position their shooters at the edge of the circle ready to fire in.

- The aim of the game is to knock the opponent's marbles out of the circle. If playing for 'keeps', the player who knocks the marble out keeps it. To start with, I'd suggest just playing for fun, where the knocked-out marble is kept to the side and used to monitor the score.

- To knock out an opponent's marble, simply flick the shooter towards the target. If the player manages to hit it but doesn't knock it out, they get to try again until they miss entirely. If the shooter rolls out of the circle, it moves on to being the next player's turn.

- If a player manages to knock their opponent's shooter out of the circle, they win all the marbles that player has won so far.

- If the shooter is outside the circle when it comes back to being a player's go, they simply place it on the edge of the circle to fire it in. If it remained in the circle, they fire it from wherever it is.

- Play ends when all a player's marbles are knocked out, making the other player the winner.

Helicopter Ride

What's the game?

This game was invented by my boyfriend's dad. It's a much-anticipated feature of the Girling family Christmas and has the kids clamouring for their turn every year. It involves taking the child on a mock helicopter ride and provides the exhilarating feeling of lifting high into the air when they're actually only two feet off the ground.

One of the now-famous Brit artists did something similar several years ago at an art event. It involved them standing a gallery visitor in front of their sculpture of a miniature landscape, grabbing them around the waist, lifting them a few centimetres off the ground and shouting, 'Look at the little cows and sheep and hedgerows in the field below!'

What do I need to play it?

A chair, a book and a blindfold.

How many kids and what age?

You need four people in total for each ride: one passenger (the child) and ideally three adults to help out. This one will appeal to children aged four and over.

How do I play it?

- Blindfold the first passenger and stand them on a chair.

- Two adults stand either side of the chair and the passenger places their hands on the heads of the two lifters to steady themselves.

- A commentary is then provided as the helicopter 'takes off' and travels high up into the clouds: 'We will shortly be departing from Chair Airport. Please ensure your safety belt is fastened. We will be travelling upwards at a gentle speed before heading off across the living room.'

- As the commentary is given, the two people either side of the chair lift it about ten centimetres off the ground while simultaneously bending their knees and lowering their heads. This does take a small degree of strength.

- This gives the child the exhilarating feeling that they're lifting off high into the sky. The commentary continues: 'You are now flying over the green hills. There's a farmyard below with some cows and sheep in the fields. We're now going to travel much higher . . .'

- As you say this, someone steps behind the child and slowly lowers a large hardback book onto their head to give the feeling that they've hit the ceiling. At this point the child can take their blindfold off and they'll be mightily surprised that they're actually so close to the ground.

- The other way you can end the ride is to ask the child to jump off the chair before removing the blindfold. There have been a few tears with this route, however, so it may be better to stick to the book option.

Murder in the Dark

What's the game?

This is a macabre classic that has multiple variations. I've featured the one we used to play when we were children, as I think it's fairly close to the original form. We used to love this game, particularly as it allowed us to scream and gurgle in agony as we writhed and wriggled to our gruesome deaths.

The game involves everyone drawing cards to find out if they're the 'murderer', 'victim' or 'detective' and then running around in the dark acting out their roles. My brother once tricked us all by secretly doctoring the papers so that everyone was the murderer. The sound emitted from our house that night was akin to an evening in a Victorian prison.

What do I need to play it?

A hat, a pen, some paper and a very dark room or rooms.

How many kids and what age?

You need a minimum of four kids aged eight and over. To play the court case part of the game, children really need to be aged ten or above.

How do I play it?

- First of all, sort through a deck of cards and pull out an ace, a jack, a king, a queen and number cards for the amount of remaining players.
- Next, get all the players to discreetly choose a card from the pack. All the cards have a meaning and you need to let the players know who they are while making sure they don't tell anyone else: the ace is the murderer, the jack is the detective, the king is the detective if the jack dies, and the queen is the detective if the jack and the king both die. The number cards are other potential victims.
- Once everyone knows who they are, collect the cards and put them to the side for the next game.

- Next, turn off all the lights so that it's completely dark and get everyone to spread out through the house as quietly as possible. You may need to encourage some of the kids to leave their friends as it's important that everyone disappears on their own.
- And this is where the anarchy begins to take shape. Victims are trying to avoid the murderer, the murderer is trying to commit the crime and the detective is trying to figure out what the barnacles is going on.
- When the murderer finds one of their victims, they need to tap them on the shoulder and the victim must immediately fall down to the floor, either silently or making as much noise as possible.
- When another player comes across a person lying still on the ground, they ask 'Are you dead?' The person has to tell the truth by nodding or shaking their head. If they say yes, the person who found them shouts, 'Murder in the Dark!'
- At this point the lights go on, the game stops and everyone returns to the room they started in.
- Next, the game moves into the courtroom, where the detective sits in a chair with the victims sat on the floor behind him and all the other players on the floor in front. If the detective (the person who picked the jack card) has been murdered, the person who picked the king card takes over as the detective. If both those with the jack and king cards have been murdered, the person who picked the queen card acts as detective.
- The detective must now try to work out who the murderer is by putting lots of questions to each person. The questions should be along the lines of 'Where were you when "Murder in the Dark!" was called?' or 'What have you got to say in your defence?' or 'Who do you think the murderer is?'
- When the detective has completed their investigations, they must make an informed guess as to who they think the murderer is. If asked if they are the murderer, it is vital that players answer the question truthfully.
- A winning murderer is one who avoids being identified until the bitter end.

When You're *Stuck Indoors* 47

The Silhouette Game

What's the game?

This is actually a Victorian parlour game which will have
the kids in stitches. I've played this many a time with
adults, though it's fairly easy to guess who's who and
it's the silhouetted performance that provides the most
entertainment.

What do I need to play it?

A strong torch and a sheet, and somewhere to suspend the
sheet from. This is also one to play in a darkened room,
as you need the lack of light to create the silhouettes with
torches.

How many kids and what age?

You need at least six of them to make the guessing part
work. You'll also need up to four adults: two to hold the
sheet, if you can't hang it, one to hold the torch and the
other to run the guessing game on the other side. This one
works best with children aged seven and over.

How do I play it?

- First of all, you need to set up your room by finding somewhere to hang your sheet so that it's suspended like a curtain all the way down to the floor (this is crucial to prevent any shoes giving the game away). If you can't find a way of doing this, then you'll need two adults to stand on chairs and hold the sheet up so that it hangs down to the floor.

- Next, you need to test your apparatus to ensure that you can get your room dark enough and that your torch is strong enough to create a silhouette.

- Once you're ready to go, get the children to split into two teams. The first team goes out of the room to a spot from where they can easily access the back of the sheet, while the others stay in the room.

- The children from the first team then take it in turns to go behind the sheet with the torch shining behind them to create their silhouette. They must then silently dance or create funny shapes while the children from the other team try to guess who it is.

- They get three guesses and, if guessed correctly, the child then reveals themselves.

- The game plays on until all children are identified and the teams then swap places.

Pig

What's the game?

Pig is great fun to play with adults and kids and will easily while away a rainy afternoon. It's a card game that works well in big groups as well as small, and it's one that's really easy for kids to pick up.

What do I need to play it?

A pack of cards.

How many kids and what age?

Works well in groups of four, but lots of fun for larger groups of up to thirteen. Kids should ideally be aged seven and over.

How do I play it?

- First count out four of the same number or face card for each player. It doesn't matter which ones you choose, as the different cards have no intrinsic value.

- Once sorted, discard the remainder of the deck, shuffle the pack and deal them out so that everyone has four cards each.

- The aim of each round is to be the first to collect a matching set of four cards.

- To start play, the dealer says 'Go' and players simultaneously choose their least favourite card (the one that seems least likely to lead to a matching set of four) and place it face down on their left-hand side. Players then pick up the card the person to their right has laid down. If it matches anything in their hand, they should probably keep it; if not, it might be one they choose to discard on the next turn.

- The dealer then says 'Go' again and players continue putting down a card before picking up the one that's placed to their right. Play continues until someone gets four matching cards.

- As soon as someone gets a set of four matching cards, they put their finger on the tip of their nose. On seeing this, all players must copy the action. Whoever's last to do so earns a letter 'P' for Pig. If a player is last a second time, they get a letter 'I', and so on.

- The first player to earn the letters P-I-G is out, and one of the sets of four cards is removed from play before the game plays on. Play continues in the same way until only one player is left in and is declared the winner.

Trumps

What's the game?

Trumps, or Knockout as it is also known, was a family favourite in our household when I was a nipper. I can remember huddling by the fire for hours listening intently as our dad taught us the art of the game. Before long we were hooked and became obsessed with playing at any opportunity. Under bedcovers at midnight or at the crack of dawn before school, we could be found shuffling and dealing like card sharps with a hustler's twinkle in our eyes. Thankfully, like any new toy, the interest eventually wore off and no subsequent gambling addictions developed.

The aim of the game is to win as many of the seven rounds as possible by winning the most 'tricks' in each round.

What do I need to play it?

A pack of cards.

How many kids and what age?

The maximum number of players is seven, but it works best in groups of four to five. Players should be aged seven and upwards.

How do I play it?

- Nominate one player as the dealer. The role of dealer passes clockwise around the players after each round.

- To get started, the dealer shuffles the pack and deals out seven cards to each of the players, dealing him or herself last. The aim of the game is to win the most 'tricks' in the seven rounds, i.e. the cards that are laid down in each round of play. To win a trick, you must lay down the highest card number or the highest trump card. Trumps

are the suit worth more than any other in that round.

- To decide which suit is trumps, the top card from the undealt pack is turned upwards; the suit of that card is trumps.

- The player to the left of the dealer leads by placing a card face upwards with the other players doing the same thing in a clockwise direction. Players must follow suit if possible; if they can't, they should play a trump; if they have no trumps, any card can be used. Once everyone has laid a card, the highest card of the suit that was laid first wins that trick, however, if someone played a trump, the highest trump wins.

- Once no one has any cards left, the first round is completed. The winner of the most tricks wins the round. The cards are collected by the dealer, who then deals out six cards to each player and the game plays on in the same fashion with the winner of the previous round nominating trumps.

- If a player doesn't win any tricks in a round, they're out of play. Each round is played out until the last round, when the remaining players have one card each.

- If a round is drawn, the deck is cut and the drawing players pick a card. The player who selects the highest card, irrespective of suit, wins the right to nominate trumps.

- The winner is the last person left in the game, or the winner of the final one-trick round.

Turkey Truss

What's the game?

This one is very amusing to watch. You need to ensure the kids take care not to bash each other too much, as it's one where they can get easily carried away.

What do I need to play it?

Two ropes or scarves, and two walking sticks or broomsticks or umbrellas.

How many kids and what age?

You need two to battle and the rest to watch. I'd suggest playing it with children aged seven and over.

How do I play it?

- First of all, choose which children are going to play and then prepare them for their duel.
- With the children sitting on the floor, you need to tie each child's ankles together with ropes or scarves, position the stick or umbrella under their knees and get them to bend their knees up to their chests.
- Next, get them to hook their elbows under the umbrella and clasp their hands, still with elbows bent, up in front of them as if in prayer.
- When securely positioned, move each child so that they're facing each other with toes touching.
- On the word 'Go!', the children battle to try to knock the other over by using their feet to flip the other child off balance. Keep an eye out to make sure the ends of the sticks don't jab the other child.
- The rule is that knees and elbows must remain bent to ensure the child maintains their trussed-up position.
- A tournament format can be created where simultaneous games are played, ending in a final turkey-trussing battle.

Make Your Own Fun

Look of the Season

What's the game?

This one's perfect for aspiring fashion designers or anyone with a bit of creative flair. It was born out of a birthday weekend in a thatched cottage in the countryside. It culminated in a fully commentated fashion show, with all of us wearing the winner's new designs for the rest of the evening.

What do I need to play it?

Whatever you can lay your hands on – bin bags, kitchen roll, curtains, sheets, bath mat, feather duster – you get the idea.

How many kids and what age?

As many kids as you like, aged six and upwards. I'd suggest no more than four players in each team.

How do I play it?

- Players get into teams and are given a set amount of time to go away and design an outfit from whatever they can lay their hands on.

- The only rule is that actual clothing is banned. Outfits need to be customised from whatever can be found around the house. You can choose to have one model with the rest of the group creating, or you might opt to have the whole team wearing a collection of the inspired creations.

- Points should be awarded for creativity and inspired accessorising.

Three

Creative
'Make and Do'
Fun

'Make and do', as kids' crafts have become fondly known, is an inspired way to keep your kids amused, while encouraging them to explore and develop their creative prowess.

To prevent your home being turned into an eccentric artist's studio of dubious talent, there are a few things you can do to make your kids' crafting manageable. Firstly, assign a dedicated creativity area. If it's warm outside, the garden or even the garden shed is an ideal choice. If it's wet and miserable or you're lacking in the outdoor space department, designate a craft area in your home and lay down some strict rules about where and when it can happen.

Secondly, be prepared. The brilliant thing about make and do is that it can be rolled out at any time of the day and with however many kids you're looking after. It's ideal for one or for an after-school gang. To maximise its potential, you need to have a stash of crafting materials in a drawer or box that can be pulled out whenever the moment arises. This doesn't mean you need to stock up on expensive materials from your local art shop; it means you need to start being canny about what you hold on to. Milk-bottle tops, old Christmas cards and wrapping paper, cardboard boxes, bits of ribbon and interesting food packaging are all worth keeping in your craft box.

This chapter is packed full of creative ideas and inspiration to help unleash the future Hockney or Hirst, Rowling or Ballard in your young charge.

Puppet Show

What's the activity?

Kids are natural puppeteers. From an early age you will find them animating the characters in their toy box and giving them different voices and personalities.

One of my most memorable holidays was the Christmas when we decided to create our own puppet theatre and mark New Year's Day with a specially choreographed show. We spent a good fortnight crafting our characters and arguing over the script, only to have the whole thing ruined by a sibling spat. I was left having to operate my sister's snake as well as my own maiden and the prince who was supposed to be defending her from the serpent's jaws. It all ended in a bit of a tangled mess, but, spats aside, it afforded us a cherished fortnight of creating and crafting that had us utterly absorbed in our own worlds.

There are lots of different ways you can make puppets, depending on the time and resources you have. I've included some different ideas on how to make different puppet types, along with a suggestion as to how to craft the theatre to perform in.

How many kids and what age?

This is great to entertain as large or as small a group of kids as you have. It can also be scaled up and down in complexity to suit all ages.

How to make a caterpillar puppet

- This one only requires two sheets of A3 paper (one green and one yellow would be ideal), a stick from the garden, some string and some sticky tape, and a pipe cleaner if you've got one to make the antennae.

- First of all, cut the sheets of paper into four-centimetre-wide strips and give the child one of each colour.

- Next, get them to stick the ends of two strips together to create a right angle. Once firmly stuck in place, get them to alternate folding the strips of paper over each other to create a corrugated tower structure. If you want to make your caterpillar longer, then simply make another tower and stick the two pieces together.

- Next, cut out a large circle to make the head and stick this to one end of the tower. Cut out two white circles with two smaller black circles inside to create the eyes. Alternatively, get the child to draw on the features.

- Then take your pipe cleaner, cut two small pieces off and tape these to the back of the head, positioning them so that they curl forward.

- Finally, tape or staple a piece of string to the front and the back of the caterpillar and then tie the other ends to the stick to give you a handle to move the puppet about.

How to make a sock puppet

- It's easy to animate a sock puppet and give it loads of character. All you need are some clean old socks, a couple of buttons, a needle and thread and any other material or wool you have lying around to make the eyes and outfit. Felt is an ideal material to make ears and other features.

- First of all, get the child to decide on what kind of creature they'd like to craft. It might inspire them if you put the sock on their hand and show them how to stick their thumb in the heel to animate the mouth.

- Sew the buttons in place on the sock to create the eyes. It might be a good idea for an adult to do this part if the child is quite young.

- Finally, it's all about adding features and clothes to give the puppet character. You might want to show them how they can cut out felt ears and noses, or how to give their puppet a collar and tie or a simple dress. And you're done – simple.

Make Your Own Fun

How to make a finger puppet

- If you're looking for a quick-fix puppet, this is probably the easiest to put together and allows kids to take the lead on drawing their characters.

- All you need is some card and some colourful pens. If you've got the time, you can use felt, old material or coloured pieces of paper to create the characters' outfits.

- With these puppets, get your kids to draw and colour in their puppet character down to the top of their legs. Then cut them out, leaving a large area at the bottom where you'll need to cut two child's-finger-sized holes for the kids to stick their fingers through and create some dancing legs.

- Done!

How to make a prince or princess puppet

- A great way to make a person puppet is to use a wooden spoon. If you can't spare one from your kitchen, they're really cheap to buy if you avoid the posh kitchen shops. They're great things to have handy to inspire some rainy-afternoon crafting.

- You'll also need some old material to create the clothes, some wool for the hair and some thick felt-tip pens to draw on the features.

- The basic idea is that the spoon part becomes the head and the stick part the body. The stick is cloaked in an outfit allowing for a discreet place for the hand to hold the puppet.

- This is another one where the kids can take the lead in crafting it all together, gluing the material in place to create the outfits and the wool on the spoon head to create the hair and then using the felt-tip pens to draw in the features.

How to make an animal puppet on a stick

- Another puppet-making technique that also uses a wooden spoon is to put a sock over the top of the spoon and stuff things in the toe of the sock to create an animal face. Plastic cups are great to create the long nose of a dog, horse or cow, or use a diamond-shaped piece of card which when folded in half and stuffed in the toe can be used to create a bird's beak.

- You can then use buttons for the eyes and felt features to finish it off.

How to make a puppet theatre

- After all this creative crafting, you need to ensure the kids have somewhere decent to show off their work. This is where the puppet theatre comes in.

- You can make this as elaborate as you like, or if they're old enough, give the kids the materials they need and leave them to do the work.

- The easiest format is to use a large sturdy cardboard box or crate, ideally about a metre square. Remove the bottom and then flip up one of the flaps and fix it in place.

- This provides your basic structure; now it's all about covering it in material to create a theatre-like shape.

- If you've got the time, you can also get the kids to make curtains by cutting out some material and folding the top over and then stitching this into place. You then need to thread your material onto a long piece of string, which is then tied into place at the inside top of the theatre structure by piercing two holes in the side and tying a couple of decent knots.

Recycle-Bin Sculpture

What's the activity?

Creative crafting from the contents of your recycling bin needn't be confined to *Blue Peter* viewers. An afternoon on a rug in the garden recreating the Angel of the North can be mightily entertaining.

How many kids and what age?

Great for all ages and for groups of kids of all sizes.

What do I need?

A selection of packaging and odds and sods from your recycling bin, scissors, tape, string, some of those gold pins with the folding arms and some good old-fashioned glue.

What do we do?

- Gather a good collection of recyclable bits, around four to five for each player.

- On the word 'Go!', players scramble to collect their chosen pieces and head off to get crafting. I'd suggest putting a time limit on this event, or if you're looking for masterpieces, perhaps the judging could form part of the end-of-weekend awards ceremony.

- The selection of winners is based on whatever criteria you feel are most appropriate to your group.

Fishing

What's the activity?

This is a great one to have in the cupboard ready to roll out when you've got a handful of grizzling kids stuck inside due to the rain. It takes a little preparation, but that's half the fun.

What do I need?

To do a proper job on this, you really need to make a trip to your local DIY shop. Alternatively, you can fashion most of the elements from the contents of your recycling bin:

- Wooden dowling (a few strong twigs should suffice).
- Some string.
- Screw-in hooks.
- Small offcuts of wood.
- Acrylic paint and other waterproof bits and pieces for decoration.
- Something to make your pond; a washing-up bowl is ideal.

How many kids and what age?

However many you have to hand. Works for children aged five and over.

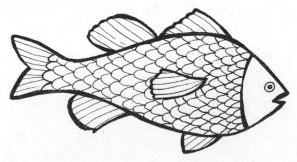

What do we do?

- First of all, you need to create your fishing rods. Take your twig or wooden dowling and cut to about half a metre long, then securely attach a piece of string with a loop tied into one end.

- Next, you need to fashion your fish using your offcuts of wood. You can be as creative as you like with this; definitely have a rumble in your recycling bin for decorative bits. We cut up a pile of those shiny crisp wrappers and looped and taped them to form elaborate fins and tails. Don't forget to attach a large hook to its topside.

- Once rod and fish are ready, simply set them afloat in your pond and start fishing. You can assign different points to different fish to add a competitive element to the game.

- It's a good idea to let the children take it in turns rather than having a free-for-all – it'll only end up in tears and tangled rods.

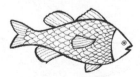

Garden Sculptures

What's the activity?

No matter how hard we try, humans just aren't able to equal the majesty that exists in the world outside. Encouraging children to see the wonder in the furls of fern fronds or autumn's colour palette is a sure-fire way to nurture their love of the great outdoors. Making a sculpture out of twigs, leaves, branches and even mud will entertain your young charges for most of the afternoon.

What do I need?

A good collection of whatever you can find in the garden. This activity is a great way to entertain the kids while you're doing some pruning or garden clearing, as you can pass them your offcuts to craft with: leaves, branches, lawn clippings, petals, pebbles – they'll be able to use whatever you find.

How many kids and what age?

Great for kids of all ages and groups of all sizes.

What do we do?

- Get your kids set up somewhere that's not going to ruin your garden. Lay out their approved selection of garden offcuts and get them crafting. Below are a couple of ideas to help inspire their creations:
  - Grass cuttings for hair.
  - Petals for clothes.
  - Sticks for arms and legs.
  - Painted pebbles for eyes.
  - Long leaves for clothes.
- If your kids are particularly creative, you could get them to create a hanging sculpture by weaving flexible twigs into a shape and wrapping leaves and cuttings in between.

Creative *Make and Do* Fun

Vegetable Friends

What's the activity?

I always have a few faded and shrivelled specimens at the bottom of my vegetable drawer. Rather than berating yourself for your failure as a domestic god or goddess, give a new lease of life to these inedible roots and get your kids to create a village of vegetable friends.

What do I need?

Some fading root vegetables – carrots, potatoes, parsnips – anything that has a firm structure to it. You'll also need some extra bits and pieces to create the features and outfits – felt, pipe cleaners, old material, spaghetti, coloured dough (see 'Dough You Know What It Is?' on page 142 for a recipe for salt dough). Be creative and use whatever you've got to hand. Oh, and you also need some glue to stick bits into place.

How many kids and what age?

Great for kids of all ages in groups large and small.

What do we do?

- Gather your collection of crafting materials and get stuck in. Below are some ideas of how you can create your vegetable friends:

  - Pipe cleaners are great to use for arms and legs as they can be stuck into the vegetable.

  - Old material can be cut into shapes to make vegetable-friend clothes. Keep them as simple as possible, such as a thin piece for a skirt or a waistcoat with holes cut out for the pipe-cleaner arms.

  - Play dough or salt dough can be used to make features and clothing items.

  - Spaghetti can be snapped into smaller sticks and stuck into the top of the vegetable to create hair.

- After the kids are done with their crafting, the vegetable friends could become residents of the breakfast village, neatly leading onto the next activity – see the following page.

The Breakfast Village

What's the activity?

This one is called the Breakfast Village because it involves crafting a village using the leftover packaging from your breakfast.

What do I need?

Collect together the debris from your breakfast table: milk cartons (a few of these of different sizes if possible), cereal packets, egg cartons. Then you'll need a whole load of bits to decorate the houses: coloured paper, ribbon, corrugated cardboard, felt-tip pens and pictures of windows and doors cut out of magazines. If you want to decorate your village, you can create trees, flowers and even people using salt dough (see page 142 for the recipe). As with all these activities, it's about using up what you can get your hands on. Finally, you'll need glue and scissors to cut and stick it all in shape.

How many kids and what age?

Great for kids of all ages in large and small groups. Younger children will need more help.

What do we do?

- To make your house, simply follow the steps below:

  - Get some coloured paper and cover your milk carton all over as if it's a brightly coloured house.

  - Cut out some pictures of windows, doorways, plants and pots from some gardening or home magazines and stick these into place.

  - Finally, create your roof by sticking some firmer card or corrugated card on the top to create a pitched roof. Brown felt is another great roof alternative, especially if your glue isn't strong enough to stick the card in place.

- To make a block of flats or factory, you can use a cereal packet instead, but this time keep the square shape and follow the steps above.

- Egg boxes are great cut up and used as plant pots or rubbish bins; screwed-up bits of tin foil can make railings; strips of black and white paper make great zebra crossings. As always, it's about using what you've got in your recycling box or around the house, rather than having to go out and buy something new.

Egg-Carton Monsters

What's the activity?

This is one of my favourite pieces of make and do for kids. It quickly turns the humble egg carton into a truly realistic and scary monster.

What do I need?

An egg carton for each child, scissors, glue, and red, green, white and blue felt or paper.

How many kids and what age?

Great for kids of all ages in groups large and small. It's a bit fiddly for the younger ones, so you'll need an adult on hand to help.

What do we do?

- First of all, you need to create your monster shape. Carefully tear the lid off the egg carton so that you have two separate parts, and also detach the smaller flap from the lid that is used to hold the carton closed – don't throw this away as you'll need it later.

- Next, you need to cut the bottom part of the egg carton in half down the middle of the tray, to create the teeth. An adult will probably need to do this bit, as it's quite tricky manoeuvring scissors in between the egg holders.

- Once you've done this, put lots of glue in the egg-carton lid and position the two egg-carton halves in the lid so that they appear like big scary monster teeth. You may need to trim the sides of the egg holders to ensure they fit in.

- To complete your monster shape, you then take the smaller flap that is normally used to hold the egg carton closed and cut two eye shapes in it, leaving a length at the bottom of each to stick these in place. Put some glue on the length and stick these in the two holes that normally hold the egg carton closed. If possible, it's a good idea to set your carton aside at this point to leave it to dry.

- Finally, it's the fun bit. Cut out a red tongue and stick this in between the teeth as if the monster is poking its tongue out. Next, cut some white and black circles and stick these in place to create the eyes; you could even add some eyelashes if you fancy it. Then cut out a long zigzag tail and stick it on the back of the egg carton, plus some tentacle-like hands sticking out of the side.

- All done! All you need to do now is come up with a name.

Ice Art

What's the activity?

This is a fun activity to do in winter when you can be guaranteed a frosty night. Alternatively, it's a great way to create some novelty ice cubes in your freezer for a summer's day.

What do I need?

You'll need some sort of shallow and flexible dish – empty margarine tubs are great, or plastic food containers work just as well. You'll also need to choose an item from the garden that you'd like to frame in ice, and a twig and string to create the hole and bit to hang it from.

If you're creating summer ice cubes, you need an ice-cube tray and an item to feature in your ice cubes, such as mint leaves, slices of strawberry or curls of lemon rind. Make sure you choose something that's going to end up tasting nice when it's swimming around in someone's drink.

How many kids and what age?

Great for kids of all ages and all group sizes.

How to make winter ice art

- This is really easy to do. Simply get the kids to choose some items they think are beautiful enough to frame in ice and lay them flat in the container before covering with water. Finally, lean the twig in so that when it freezes it leaves a sort of hole. Do as many of these as you have containers available.

- Pop them outside for the night, away from the house to ensure they get as cold as possible, and leave them until the next morning.

- After a chilly night you should be able to turn out some beautiful ice pendants. Wiggle your twig around to carefully remove it without cracking the ice. You might need to poke it about a bit so it breaks through to the other side. It's a good idea to have a few ice pendants made up in case this bit goes wrong.

- Next, thread a piece of string through the hole and then get your kids to decorate a tree near your house. These should last for as long as the temperature stays low.

How to make some summer-fun ice cubes

- Choose your piece of fruit or item you'd like frozen into the ice cubes and get the kids to carefully place one in each of the ice-cube trays before covering them in water and placing in the freezer.

- After a few hours or the next morning, pop them out and stick them in the kids' drinks.

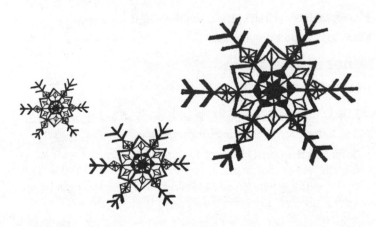

Crime-Scene Sketches

What's the activity?

My friend Johnno is that brilliant Boy Scout type of guy who always has the right kit, along with a plethora of ideas to keep his kids, young Grace and William, entertained. This is an ace activity he came up with and one he's rolled out on many a rainy day. It gets the kids to produce self-portraits that when collected together year on year provide a fantastic record of their development.

What do I need?

Some old wallpaper or lining paper and a collection of pens, paints and any collage materials (old bits of material, wool, milk-bottle tops or wrapping paper, for example) that you can rustle up.

How many kids and what age?

Ideal for all kids of all ages.

What do we do?

- Lay out all your collage materials, paints and pens on the floor. This has the potential to get quite messy if your kids get carried away in their artistic endeavours, so you may want to put some newspaper down underneath.

- Cut a length of wallpaper for each child, ensuring that it is slightly longer than them in length. Next, get the child to lie down on the sheet of wallpaper and draw around them using a thick marker to create an outline of their shape.

- Now the fun begins. Get the kids to create an image of themselves using pens, paints and all the collage materials you have collected together.

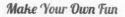 *Make Your Own Fun*

Cobweb Pictures

What's the activity?

Cobwebs are one of nature's secret treasures. I can remember one school assembly when a teacher displayed a cobweb she'd collected on a bent twig on the way to work for us all to marvel at. The way she spoke about how the dew hung from it like crystals sparkling in the sunlight created a fascination with these webby structures that's always remained with me.

You can encourage your kids to marvel at the beauty of a cobweb by showing them how to create this Cobweb Picture.

What do I need?

Talcum powder, black paper and spray-on glue or hairspray.

How many kids and what age?

Great for kids of all ages and all group sizes.

What do we do?

- First of all, get your kids to go out and hunt down their cobweb. Ideally try and choose an old abandoned one. If you do decide to use an inhabited one, just make sure the spider is well away from home.

- Next, spray the cobweb all over with the hairspray or spray-on glue and then puff on some talcum powder before sealing it with your spray again.

- Position the black paper behind the cobweb and pull the sheet of paper towards you so that the cobweb is released from its home and rests on your sheet. Leave the sheet to dry overnight before hanging it somewhere for you all to enjoy.

Pandemonium

What's the activity?

Kids love to make a racket. While this can be frustrating, giving them permission to create noise in a controlled way enables you to limit the damage to your mental well-being.

What do I need?

Get your kids to decide what they are going to use. This is all about encouraging your kids to explore the different sounds that can be created from household paraphernalia. Think saucepans, old paint tins, wooden spoons – see below for some more ideas.

How many kids and what age?

Great for small groups of kids aged five and upwards.

What do we do?

- Below are a few inspirations to help your kids on their way:
  - Scratching a wooden spoon down a cheese grater makes an interesting percussion instrument.
  - Lentils in a jar is another addition to the percussion set.
  - A couple of empty paint tins and a couple of wooden spoons make ideal drums.
  - Create a guitar by stretching some elastic bands over a tissue box.
  - Create a rain stick by putting dried rice or lentils in a postal tube and sealing it at both ends and then banging in a series of short nails to slow down the progress of the pulses as they move down the tube to create a rain-like sound.

Make Your Own Fun

Bloomin' Marvellous

What's the activity?

This is a really simple activity that's also a great way to teach your kids some basics in botany. Flowers can be made to change to a colour of your choosing by adding a few drops of food colouring to their water and leaving them overnight. Daffodils and white carnations are good ones to use. If you haven't got flowers to hand, celery sticks are brilliant for creating the same magical effect.

Mr Grassy Head

What's the activity?

Mr Grassy Head will provide much entertainment as you watch this character's hair slowly grow. Once it gets to a certain length, you can experiment with different grassy styles.

What do I need?

For this activity you need an old stocking, some compost, some grass seed, an old cup, some brown cotton, some different-coloured felt to create the features and some scissors and glue to stick them on.

How many kids and what age?

Great for small groups of kids aged five and upwards.

What do we do?

- First of all, cut off the foot of your stocking, including about ten centimetres of the leg.
- Next, put a generous handful of grass seed into the toe of the sock, before filling up the rest of the foot of the stocking with compost and tying the rest of the stocking in a knot to hold it all in place.
- You can then create a nose by squeezing it into shape and tying it in place with some cotton.
- Now you're ready to cut out and stick on Mr Grassy Head's features using the felt.
- Finally, put some water in the cup and position the head firmly in the cup so that the water soaks through the compost and up to the seed.
- Position on a bright windowsill and watch the grass locks grow.

Scarey-Crow

What's the activity?

Getting your kids to make a scarecrow is a great way to keep them entertained while you get on with some gardening.

What do I need?

Some old clothes, a hat, two garden canes or long, straight branches, string, some straw, thick tape, a paper bag and some thick felt-tip pens to draw on the features.

How many kids and what age?

Great for kids of all ages and all group sizes.

What do we do?

- Make a cross using the two garden canes or branches to give the scarecrow its basic structure and then stuff the brown paper bag with straw and tape it to the top of the cane to create the scarecrow's head. Finish it off by drawing on some features.

- Next, dress your scarecrow by putting the clothes on your cane structure and then stuff these full of straw before tying off the arms and legs to keep it all in.

- Finally, stick the cane firmly in the ground so that he can get on with his scarecrowing work.

Four

Fun for
Holidays

Holidays are made for kids. It's a time for them to enjoy lazy mornings and late nights, sandy escapades and outdoor adventures, only to return with scraped knees and blackberry-smeared mouths. Holidays are a time of freedom and indulgence, and until your kids retire, it's the last chance they'll get to sit around licking a lolly and pondering why the grass is green. Unless of course they go to university.

The reality of holidays is often less idyllic. Rain-sodden tents or too much time in each other's company can sometimes lead to squabbles and grumps that put a dampener on proceedings. The following chapter is teeming with ideas for holiday fun to keep everyone happy. Whether it's frolicking on the beach or lazing by the pool, this chapter's got enough homespun fun to save you lugging half your toy box with you and will save you a packet on excess baggage.

Beach Monsters

What's the game?

We came up with the game of beach monsters on our favourite beach in Wales a couple of years ago when some young cousins joined our camping holiday. After discovering the hilarity that could be had from sticking round shells in your eye sockets and surprising people with our scary faces, we decided to take it one step further and fashion ourselves an entire beach-find costume and run around like strange ghostly seafarers returned from the dead (well, that's what we liked to think anyway).

You need to be fairly un-squeamish for this game as it does involve kids sticking seaweed down their swimming costume and in their hair.

What do I need to play it?

Some enthusiastic and un-squeamish kids and a beach to play on.

How many kids and what age?

As many or as few as are there. Great for all ages.

How do I play it?

- Get your kids to plan their outfit based on what they can find on the beach. Then get them to customise their look with seaweed and shell finds.

- They could create a seaweed skirt by tucking the seaweed in their swimming costumes or a seaweed cape by draping it down their backs and over their arms. Shells stuck in eye sockets is also a good look, and if they really want to get stuck in they can jump in the sea and roll themselves around in the sand until they're completely covered before accessorising with seaweed and shells.

Beach Volcano

What's the activity?

This is less of a game and more of a challenge. It's a great one to play with kids to fill a long lazy afternoon on the sands. A competitive element could of course be built in, for example rewarding the longest-smoking volcano, or the last one standing when the tide comes in. A word of warning should be added: kids will definitely need adult supervision with this one and please, please ensure that all fires are completely put out and that materials are fully cleared away.

What do I need?

Sand, sculpting hands, some kindling and a lighter.

How many kids and what age?

As few or as many as you like. Suitable for all ages but for safety's sake kids should really be aged five and over, and an adult is needed to make sure things don't get out of hand.

What do we do?

- Make a pile of sand, funnel a hole in the middle down to the ground and then funnel in from the side until your two passages meet.

- Decorate the outside, really getting creative – seaweed for grass and bushes, colourful eruptions, and so on.

- Then push some paper or driftwood into the bottom of your passage and light a long dry twig that is then used to light the driftwood and paper that's inside the volcano. Smoke should soon billow from the top like an exploding volcano. To complete the apocalypse, you should time it so the tide comes in once the eruption has had some time to show off. This will make sure the volcano is fully extinguished before you leave the beach.

Make Your Own Fun

Sand-Sculpture Competition

What's the activity?

Sand sculpting is an art played out on beaches around the world. Even the sandy banks of the Thames regularly play host to such artists.

A friend came across a sand-sculpture competition on a Dorset beach where the most fantastically imaginative objects were being created. A young Hugh Fearnley-Whittingstall, later to become the celebrity chef, was an enthusiastic participant. Rather than spending hours crafting his idea, he went off to do a spot of fishing. Fifteen minutes before the judging took place, he arrived back on the beach with a net full of mackerel. He proceeded to sculpt a voluptuous mermaid's tail over his legs, below his bare torso, and then got his mackerel-filled basket and decorated the tail with a glistening fishy finish. His inspired approach won him the competition and he celebrated by barbecuing his catch and sharing it with his fellow contestants.

What do I need?

Whatever flotsam and jetsam you can find to fuel your kids' imaginations and a bucket and spade.

How many kids and what age?

Great for groups of all sizes and all ages.

What do we do?

- Players are given a set amount of time to create their masterpieces. Part of that needs to be spent scouring the beach for materials.
- At the end of this time, players are judged and prizes awarded.

Sand Skittles

What's the game?

One of the oldest games in the world, the fun value of
Skittles has ensured its durability, with many references
made to the sport throughout history.

This is the same as the classic English pub game of
Skittles, but played on the beach with recycled plastic water
bottles filled with sand.

What do I need to play it?

Ten plastic water bottles filled with sand and with their lids
screwed back on, and something round and heavy to be the
ball. We've used a swede in the past, but they can be hard
to come by if you're playing in summer. A round pebble is a
great alternative. Ideally you'll need a few balls to save you
running around.

How many kids and what age?

A minimum of two players, and kids really need to be aged
five and over to properly grasp the rules.

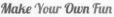
Make Your Own Fun

How do I play it?

- First up, prepare your kit. Fill your ten bottles with equal amounts of sand and screw the lids back on. If you're using a swede, give it a bit of a trim to make it as round as possible.

- Set your ten skittles up so they form an equal triangle.

- Players then have two turns to roll to see how many sand bottles they can knock down. If your ball object is lacking in roundness, you might have to adopt a throw as opposed to a roll.

- The easiest way to score is a point for every sand bottle that's knocked over.

Washing-Up-Bowl Grand National

What's the game?

For kids, racing down a hill with their bum stuck in a washing-up bowl and legs in the air is a thoroughly enjoyable way to pass an afternoon. This is another great one for the campsite, as everyone has their washing-up bowl with them. As the traditional washing-up bowl will only accommodate a small bottom, you may need to be creative in identifying alternative mounts, such as tea trays or plastic storage crates. If you're playing on sand dunes, sadly washing-up bowls tend to end up sinking into the sand. A boogie board or anything with a large flat surface is the preferred sand-dune mount.

What do I need to play it?

Ideally a washing-up bowl, but a tray would do. I've even attempted it on a bin bag, but we got a bit snagged up in the gorse.

How many kids and what age?

You need more than one to make it a race, and for safety's sake kids should really be aged seven and over.

How do I play it?

- Get everyone to the top of the hill or sand dune with washing-up bowl or designated mount in hand.
- On the word 'Go!', riders should hurtle down the hill on their mounts.
- A note as always on safety. It's wisest to avoid grassy slopes with cliffs at the end, and make sure kids practise the use of their feet as a brake. The technique is to stick your legs out forwards, enabling you to dig your heels in if needed. Not one for very young children and best if an adult keeps an eye out close by.

Make Your Own Fun

Tent Shadows

What's the game?

This one will take you back to Scout and Guide camping days. It's great fun to play if you're camping in two tents close to each other, as you can take it in turns to unzip your door and watch as the other tent do their shadow performance.

What do I need to play it?

A tent, a torch and you'll need to wait until it's dark.

How many kids and what age?

Great for groups of all sizes and ages.

How do I play it?

- Wait until it's dark outside. Show the kids how to create shapes with their hands and project these onto the tent walls using torchlight.

- Points can be awarded for creativity and how easy the shapes are to identify.

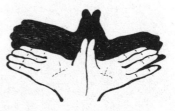

Feet-First Race

What's the game?

This game was invented one summer at my friend Nick's house in France. It was a searingly hot day, so another friend came up with a series of games to keep us entertained in the water. It's a novel way to race across the pool and will add some fun to an afternoon in the sun.

What do I need to play it?

Some kids who are strong swimmers and a pool to play in.

How many kids and what age?

As many as you can fit in a race across the pool. As always for pool games, they should be aged eight and over.

How do I play it?

- On the word 'Go!', players must swim to the other end with their legs pointing forwards and their toes poking out of the water.

- Any deviation from this position is considered a foul and players must pause for three seconds before starting to swim again.

Shark

What's the game?
This is Piggy in the Middle played in water.

What do I need to play it?
A ball and a swimming pool to play in.

How many kids and what age?
Three kids aged eight and upwards, but if there are a few more you can swap over as you go.

How do I play it?
- All three stand in the swimming pool with one in the middle and the other two either side.

- The two players either side throw the ball to each other over the head of the person in the middle.

- Meanwhile the piggy in the middle has to try to intercept the ball when it's in the air.

- If they catch it, the person who threw it then becomes the Shark in the middle.

Marco Polo

What's the game?

Marco Polo is a game of poolside 'it' that's become popular around the world. The rules will need to vary depending on the size of your pool and where it's being played, but generally it involves someone scrambling around the pool with their eyes closed trying to catch their fellow players.

The origins of the name refer to that intrepid medieval Italian explorer of the mysteries of the East.

What do I need to play it?

A swimming pool and some energetic young friends.

How many kids and what age?

A minimum of three and as many of you as can fit in the swimming pool. For safety's sake, kids really need to be aged eight and over.

How do I play it?

- Decide who's going to be 'it'. They close their eyes and count to ten, while the rest of the players scatter around the pool.

- The person who's 'it' then proceeds to swim around the pool with their eyes closed trying to catch their friends who are also moving about.

- To give a clue as to their whereabouts, the person who's 'it' can shout out 'Marco' and the rest of the players must respond with 'Polo'.

- As soon as a player is caught, it's their turn to be 'it'.

- Another variation allows players to climb out of the water when they're not 'it' to prevent them being caught. If the person who's 'it' shouts out 'Fish out of water!' while someone's out of the pool, it means the person out of the water then becomes 'it'. If there are lots of people out of the water, the person who's 'it' can choose who becomes 'it' next. If there's no one out of the water when they shout, the person who's 'it' has to do the counting part all over again.

- Another additional rule is that if the person who's 'it' shouts out 'Alligator eyes!' they're allowed to swim under the water with their eyes open to have a look at where everyone is.

Tunnel Relay Race

What's the game?

Kids who are strong swimmers and not afraid of being underwater love this game as it's a chance to show off their swimming prowess. The game involves two teams of kids racing to be the first to get their whole team to swim through a tunnel formed by their teammates' legs.

What do I need to play it?

A swimming pool to play in.

How many kids and what age?

To make it into a race you need two teams of at least three kids, though the ideal number is two teams of five. If you're playing with more than ten kids, split them into more teams. It's important to try to make sure that everyone on each team is roughly the same size so they can safely swim through the tunnel of legs. It's also important to have an adult umpire on hand to supervise the game at all times. For this game, kids should be strong swimmers aged eight and upwards.

How do I play it?

- Split the kids into teams and position them in a line somewhere in the pool so that they can safely touch the bottom where they are standing. There needs to be enough space in front of them (at the same depth) for the line to be reformed when everyone has swum through the tunnel. Get the kids to stand with their legs apart to create a tunnel. You need to ensure that when they swim through the tunnel they are far away enough from the wall that they're not going to hit their head when they come out the other side.

- When the grown-up umpire says 'Go!', the child who is at the back of the line dives down and swims through the tunnel of legs and positions himself at the top of the line. As soon as he is in place, he sticks his hand in the air to signal that it's the next child's turn to go.
- As soon as the child at the back of the line sees the hand go up in the air, they dive underwater, swim through the tunnel of legs, stand at the front and raise their hand in the air.
- The race continues until the child who went first is back at the end of the line. The first team to complete the task wins.

Rubber-Ring Polo

What's the game?

In this game players use rubber rings rather than horses and must attempt to race the ball across the pool to score goals.

What do I need to play it?

You need a floating rubber ring for each player and one beach ball. You also need bags, towels or chairs to mark out the goals at each end of the pool and the centre line.

How many kids and what age?

An ideal Rubber-Ring Polo match would have eight players and an adult acting as umpire. Kids should be strong swimmers aged eight and upwards.

How do I play it?

- To get started, mark out the centre line and the two goal areas at opposite ends of the swimming pool. Get the two teams to line up at either end in front of their goals.

- On the word, the umpire throws the ball into the middle of the pool. As soon as the ball touches the water, the teams scramble forwards to be the one to take possession. Players must stay mounted on their rubber rings at all times.

- As soon as a player takes possession, their sole objective is to chuck the ball between the goalposts of the opposition team.

- As beach balls are light, chucking it from the middle of the pool doesn't work, so players either have to manoeuvre themselves closer to the target goal or pass the ball to another player on their team who has moved into a stronger position.

- Other players can try to block the player with the ball by swimming in front of them or getting in the way of a pass, but knocking another player off their rubber ring is definitely a foul. Other fouls include any sort of physical contact with a player who has the ball or snatching of the ball from another player's hands.

- If a foul occurs or the ball is knocked out of the pool, a player on the opposite team to the one that knocked it out or caused the foul steps out of the pool and stands on the centre line and chucks the ball back in towards their chosen player.

- The winning team is the one who scores the most goals within a pre-agreed time frame.

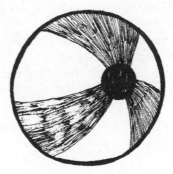

Five

Fun for *Special* *Occasions*

Christmas, Easter and bank-holiday weekends are opportunities for magical family bonding time. The following chapter fizzes with ideas for family fun throughout the year. From Pancake Day games to Christmas entertainment, there's enough inspiration here to keep your young friends thoroughly entertained.

Pancake-Day Race

What's the game?

Eating pancakes on Shrove Tuesday originates from the Christian tradition of Lent, which was marked by a forty-day fast to commemorate the death and Resurrection of Christ, culminating in a feast at Easter. Making pancakes was seen as a good way to use up any rich foods in the cupboards before the beginning of Lent.

Pancake Racing is a traditional sport played out on this auspicious Tuesday, involving a group racing each other on foot while simultaneously tossing a pancake. The most famous Pancake Race takes place at Olney and is a tradition that has been upheld for over 500 years. In 1445 a woman of Olney heard the shriving bell while she was making pancakes and ran to the church in her apron, still clutching her frying pan. This inspired an event that is honoured and observed to this day. Competitors must be female residents of the town, who should be dressed in a traditional housewife outfit. They must run the 375-metre course and perform the tossing of the pancake three times.

As I'm a bit stuffy about the idea of kids playing with and losing respect for food, I'm suggesting recreating this event for kids but with some pretend pancakes.

What do I need to play it?

You need a frying pan per racing child; try to avoid heavy iron ones if possible. You also need something to take the place of the pancake. It needs to be something that has a bit of weight to it so it can be easily flipped. If you don't have time to craft something, a small book is ideal. Finally, you also need somewhere where you can race.

How many kids and what age?

As many kids as you have that fancy getting involved.
To prevent tears resulting from unwieldy frying pans, I'd
suggest the kids are aged eight and over.

How do I play it?

- Mark out your racecourse and get your kids lined up at the
  starting line.
- On the word 'Go!', kids must race to the finishing line,
  successfully tossing the pancake three times on the way. If
  they drop the pancake on the floor, they have to go back to
  the starting line.
- First racer across the finishing line having successfully
  made their three tosses is the winner.

Easter-Egg Roulette

What's the game?

This is a great and short game to play at breakfast on Easter Day, and a brilliant way to decide who is the Treasure Hunt leader for the next game. Boil up your eggs to serve for breakfast, eat one in advance and then put all the eggs in eggcups including the shell of the eaten one, but turn this upside down so it's impossible to tell which it is. Place the eggs around the table and get the kids to choose where they're going to sit down. When they're seated, on the word 'Go!' the kids must crack their egg with a teaspoon and whoever ends up with the eaten empty egg becomes the Treasure Hunt leader. Kids find this hilarious but be warned: it's a practical joke they'll be intent on rolling out again and again.

Easter-Egg Treasure Hunt

What's the game?

The decorating and hiding of eggs for a treasure hunt on
Easter Day is an ancient Christian tradition in England
and other parts of the world. An Easter-Egg Treasure Hunt
involves laying a set of clues that lead from one to the
other before finally leading the hunters to the Easter-egg
chocolate stash.

A bit like Christmas stockings, treasure hunts are
something I've never grown out of. The tradition in our
family was that after Sunday service we would race back
home to suffer the ceremony of Easter lunch before finally
leaping from our chairs for the Easter-Egg Treasure Hunt
spectacular. Sadly, after a certain age, my aunt felt she'd
done her time as organiser and I soon picked up the mantle
to keep the tradition alive. Last year we held an Easter
Chocolate-Bunny Lamping event for some young cousins
(see page 110) and this year we hosted an aquatic Easter-Egg
Hunt on canoes that involved sunken clues and messages
swinging from overhanging branches.
The final clue was held by
the lockkeeper and led the
hunters to Duck Island to find
the chocolate Easter bounty.

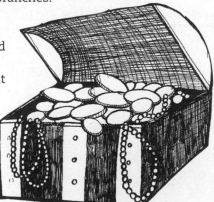

There are loads of different
ways you can do an Easter-
Egg Treasure Hunt. I've
included a couple of
ideas, but you can be
inspired by wherever
you're spending Easter to
create your own tradition.

Blown-egg clues

If you've got a bit of time and fancy being creative with your treasure hunt, you can get your kids to blow a dozen eggs and then decorate them with paint before using these as vessels to hide the clues in.

- To blow an egg, get a cocktail stick and pierce two holes, one at the bottom and one at the top. You need a small hole at the top and one about five millimetres wide at the bottom for the egg to be blown out.

- Put a bowl underneath the egg and blow through the smaller hole which should force the egg out of the bottom one. You need to make sure the kids are holding the eggs carefully to ensure they don't break. Any young ones will definitely need a hand with this.

- Next, get the kids to decorate the eggs using paints. You'll need to show them how to carefully hold and twist the egg with their index finger and thumb over the two holes to prevent the paint being smudged as they decorate.

- Once completed, leave the eggs to dry on some newspaper.

- You can then tear up some pieces of paper and write out clues that can be rolled up and poked through the larger hole, leaving a good three centimetres poking out of the top. You can now hide these eggs, saving one to hand to the hunters to mark the start of the adventure.

Balloon Treasure Hunt

Another great way to hide the Easter-egg clues, particularly for the younger kids, is to put them inside a balloon before blowing them up. The balloons are then placed around the Treasure Hunt trail and the children have to burst each one with a pin to lead them to where the next clue is hidden.

Über-super-duper Easter-Egg Treasure Hunts

For some families, the annual Easter-Egg Hunt involves much more than hunting around the garden after some well-hidden clues. I know of families that take the whole event to a quite different level, with organisers spending months in advance planning complicated trails that take up a whole afternoon and involve multiple forms of transport and the entire extended family. If you're planning an Easter spectacular for all the family to get involved in, below are some ideas of how to lay clues for an über-trail:

- If you can manage to persuade a couple of accomplices to help out, then asking someone who can be relied upon to be at a certain place at a certain time to hold a clue is a great way to add some excitement to the proceedings. Shop owners, paper boys or even the vicar at your local church are all great prospective accomplices.

- We once started our Easter-Egg Hunt by making it look as though we'd taken out an advert in the Sunday papers announcing the first clue. The ad was of course something we had created ourselves and stuck over an existing advert, but it worked as a brilliant surprise to the person who found it as they flicked through the paper over breakfast.

- If you're playing near a beach or a river, one idea is to paint a clue on the bottom of a stone (using waterproof paint), meaning the hunters have to turn over endless rocks and stones to find the next instruction.

- If you're any good at origami and are laying a trail that will take you through some garden blooms, you can create a flower out of paper with the clue hidden on it and strategically position this among the real McCoys.

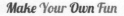

- When hunting for treasure, people always forget to look up. One year we decorated our oak tree by hanging the chocolate treasure high up in the branches, meaning the kids had to scramble up the tree to retrieve their goodies.

- If your gang are adept with a map and a compass and you're planning a hunt in the great outdoors, it's a great idea to use Ordnance Survey coordinates, combined with a cryptic clue to lead the hunters on their merry way.

- If you're playing anywhere near water and can get your hands on a floating buoy, then put a clue inside a waterproof container that you can submerge and attach to the buoy. You can direct the hunters to the clue either through Ordnance Survey coordinates or by points of reference.

Easter-Puzzle Treasure Hunts

Another great way to spice up a Treasure Hunt is to have the kids hunt down pieces of a jigsaw that when all pieced together create a map marking the location of the hidden treasure.

- First of all, you need to do a bit of preparation by drawing a map. I'd suggest using thick pens and as much colour as possible and try to use some card or thick paper to make it as easy as possible to fit together.

- Once done, cut the sheet up into jigsaw-shaped pieces and split these up into small bags or packets with a clue attached to each one.

- Lay the trail as for an ordinary Treasure Hunt but make sure pieces of the jigsaw are distributed with each of the clues. Try to split them up so that the final clue they find also features the jigsaw piece or pieces that show the actual location of the treasure.

Easter Chocolate-Bunny Lamping

What's the game?

We invented this game one Easter at a friend's house in Wales. It's best played with those gold foil-wrapped chocolate bunnies, though anything with a reflective surface works just as well. Kids love it and it's a great way to make a traditional Easter-Egg Hunt a lot more exciting.

For those not versed in the ways of the country, bunny lamping is a method that's used to catch rabbits to keep populations in check. Hunters go out with torches and shine them into rabbit-infested areas. When the light hits a rabbit, their eyes light up like bulbs, similar to when they're caught in car headlights.

What do I need to play it?

A strong torch and some foil-wrapped chocolate treats – the larger the better and at least one for every player. Oh, and a night sky.

How many kids and what age?

This requires at least one adult to plan and manage the game and as few or as many kids as you like to play. This one's suitable for all ages as long as there are some extra adults on hand to look after any very young kids.

How do I play it?

- The organiser needs to go into the garden or on a well-known walk when it's still light and hide the foil-wrapped goodies in positions where they'll shine when the torchlight hits them.

- Next, write a set of creative clues to mark out the trail. You might want to be cryptic about it. Alternatively, and especially if you're playing with young kids, you can be fairly literal, for example the clue might read 'Under a heavy green object ten paces from the front door'.

- When everything is set up and it's dark enough outside, hand a copy of the clues to each of the hunters, who then compete to find the foil-wrapped treasure by shining their torches around the directed area until a burst of gold flashes out.

Easter-Egg Roll

What's the game?

Easter-Egg Rolling is an old tradition in northern England and Scotland and is also popular in the United States. There is even a much-loved annual event that takes place on the White House lawn. The game involves contestants racing each other to be the first to roll their decorated egg across the finishing line using their nose, spoon or whatever other implement is deemed appropriate. I've outlined the nose version below as it definitely offers the most entertainment value.

What do I need to play it?

Some decorated hard-boiled eggs and a racetrack.

How many kids and what age?

Suitable for all ages and as many as you can fit along the starting line.

How do I play it?

- The day before, get the kids to decorate their hard-boiled eggs, each clearly marking their name on it to identify whose is whose.

- Get the kids lined up at the starting line, on their hands and knees with their eggs positioned in front of their noses.

- On the word 'Go!', contestants race to be the first across the finishing line, rolling their egg in front of them. Eggs must be nudged along using only the nose – strictly no hands allowed.

Apple Bobbing

What's the game?

Apple Bobbing is a fantastic Halloween game. As long as they're not afraid of water, kids love to have permission to dunk their heads and chase the apples around a bowl of water. Younger kids can find the prospect of being underwater rather scary, so you'll have to do a bit of work to persuade them it's OK.

What do I need to play it?

A big bowl that's half full of water and an apple per playing child. It's also a good idea to have some towels on hand to dry off sodden post-bobbing heads.

How many kids and what age?

This one's great for groups large or small, aged five and over.

How do I play it?

- First of all, float the apples in the bowl. Each child then puts their hands behind their back and has to retrieve an apple with their mouth.

- To add a competitive element, the event can be timed and the child who retrieves an apple in the shortest length of time wins or have more than one bowl so contestants can race each other.

Halloween Apple-Biting Contest

What's the game?

Halloween is a safe bet if you want to fire up the kids' imaginations. Whether or not you go the full hog and venture out for some Trick or Treating, there are loads of other games you can do to celebrate the day. Halloween falls at a time when there is still an abundance of home-grown apples to be had. This game involves blindfolded kids competing to take a bite from an apple swinging on a string. Ideal for Halloween parties or if someone has a birthday around this time of year.

What do I need to play it?

Some apples, a skewer, some string and somewhere to suspend the apples from. You'll also need a stopwatch, a blindfold and something to tie the kids' hands behind their backs.

How many kids and what age?

Great for kids over five, and it can be played in as large or small a group as want to get involved.

How do I play it?

- First get yourself prepared by skewering a hole down the central core of each of the apples. This should be done by an adult. Wiggle the skewer around a bit so that the string can be easily threaded through. Pull some string through and fix in place so the apple doesn't slip off.

- Hang the apples up somewhere so that the kids can reach them with their mouths. If you're lucky enough to have a lovely big tree in your garden and it's warm enough to play outside, this is a great place to hang them, otherwise you'll have to be creative with what you have available in your house.

- When the kids are ready, put a blindfold on whoever's going first and tie their hands behind their backs. On the word 'Go!', start the stopwatch. They have sixty seconds to locate one of the suspended apples and try to take a bite from it. The child who gets an apple between their teeth in the shortest time is the winner.

Old Dead Joe's Cave

What's the game?

Old Dead Joe's Cave is a popular though rather macabre American Halloween game designed to get the kids into the spooky Halloween mood by leading them through a pretend dead man's cave where they get to handle his various rotting 'body parts'. If your child is prone to nightmares or struggles to understand the difference between make-believe and reality, this is probably one to avoid. Brave and boisterous kids love it as it gives them permission to squeal with fear and delight.

What do I need to play it?

The idea behind this game is to recreate a dark cave where the rotting body parts of Old Dead Joe can be found. There are all sorts of ways you can do this, depending on what you've got handy in your cupboard. Below are some ideas and inspirations as to how to create some rotting body parts of your own (well, not actually 'your own', but you know what I mean):

- Bones: get some old steak bones from the butcher and put these on some newspaper.
- Teeth: fill a bowl with tiny hard-edged pebbles. If you can't find these, those hard corn kernels that you use to make popcorn are perfect.
- Guts: cooked and wet spaghetti or noodles in a bowl are ideal.
- Eyes: peel two grapes or kiwi fruits and place these in a smaller bowl.
- Tongue: put some raw liver in a bowl of water.

- Hair: if you've got a wig this is perfect, but you could also use a piece of sheepskin or a doll's head if you have one.

You'll also need a blindfold, a towel to wipe the kids' hands and a dark room that you can use to create the cave.

How many kids and what age?

Great for groups of any size but to save too much waiting around the ideal group size is about ten. Kids should be six and upwards to prevent them getting too frightened.

How do I play it?

- Prepare Joe's body parts by following the instructions outlined above. You'll then need to position them around a darkened room, so that you can lead the blindfolded child to touch each one.

- Once you're ready, each child takes it in turn to be blindfolded and led around Old Dead Joe's cave. As each child is led through the door and into the room you need to give a commentary. You could make up a story about what happened to poor Old Dead Joe and why he's ended up in the cave. Try to use a spooky voice as you tell the tale. The spookiness obviously needs to be tempered depending on how scared the child is.

- Once the tale is told, take the child and lead them towards each bowl and explain what they're about to touch before guiding their hands towards it.

- As soon as the child is done lead them out of the room and take off their blindfold and reassure them that it was just a game before taking them to the bathroom to wash off any goo from their hands. It's a good idea to have a towel over your shoulder as you lead each child around to wipe their hands after each 'experience' and prevent anything dripping on the floor.

Christmas-Carol Relay

What's the game?

This is a regular accompaniment to our Christmas Day preparations as we wrap our presents or stuff the turkey.

What do I need to play it?

Your best carol-singing voices and perhaps a pen and paper to keep scores.

How many kids and what age?

Ideal for two to four adults and kids. The kids need to be old enough to know the words to a good few Christmas carols.

How do I play it?

- Decide who's going first and get that person to sing a couple of lines from a popular Christmas carol.

- The others must then think of another song that features any of the words that have just been sung. For example, if I was to sing 'Silent **night**, holy night, all is calm, all is bright', then the next player might sing 'While shepherds watched their flocks by **night** all seated on the ground, the **angel** of the lord came down and glory shone around', perhaps followed by 'Hark! the herald **angels** sing, "Glory to our new-born King!"', and so on.

- Players score a point each time they correctly sing a connecting line. I'd suggest having a nominated person to keep track of scores as it's impossible to do when you're fishing Christmas carol lines from the back of your head.

Make Your Own Fun

Nature's Christmas Decorations

Christmas is a time to inspire creative youngsters into making some decorations for the home. On a wintry stomp in the countryside or your local park you should be able to find a mass of nature's material to be taken home and woven and strung up to get the kids into the spirit of the Christmas season. Some of the best decoration-making material is to be had in autumn, so I'd suggest doing your collecting when the leaves start to turn. It's a good idea to have a bit of a plan as to the sort of thing you might want to create. I've featured a few ideas below, but there is of course a wealth of stuff that you can do with whatever you find on your walk.

Autumn-leaf garlands

This one definitely needs you to get out there when the leaves are beginning to turn their autumn rainbow shades. You need to start collecting before the rains arrive and the leaves on the ground turn to a sodden sludge. This is a great way to encourage kids to get stuck into a walk by giving them a leaf-collecting activity to focus on.

Give each child a bag and instruct them each to fill it full of leaves of a certain colour, so that you end up with bags of different-coloured leaves – red, yellow, brown and so on. Place them somewhere safe to dry out for a couple of days. You want them to still be flexible to work with and not totally crunchy-crisp. Next, give each child a large needle or knitting needle with a long piece of string attached to it and instruct them to thread the end of a leaf onto the needle and down the string to create a long garland. The kids might choose to have blocks of single-coloured leaves or alternate them at random. Once done, tie a secure knot at either end and leave them somewhere safe to dry, ready to be wound around the tree or strung up when Christmas finally arrives.

Gold-leaf tree pendants

This is a great way to use up any leftover leaves that you have from your garland making, or ideal if you happen across any of those beautiful leaf skeletons that can be found once the leaf vegetation has rotted away. This time leave the leaves out so that they can fully dry. Once they're ready, an adult should spray them with gold or silver paint and carefully hang them on some thread or ribbon ready to be hung on the tree.

Conker baubles

Another one that requires advance planning as it needs you to be putting your Christmas head on as early as September, or whenever those spiky horse-chestnut shells begin to form and fall from the trees. The gathering part is really the only element the kids can get involved in, but they can 'help' you out with the rest of it. You need to try and get hold of the shells before they become too ripe and begin to open to reveal their silky insides. This might mean picking them from the trees when they're fully formed (this might not be allowed in city parks; check before you break the law). Leave them somewhere safe to dry out; this might take a couple of weeks. Once ready, you need to decide what colour you want your conker baubles (I think gold or silver works best) and then get your can of spray paint and spray them all over. Finally, get a large needle and sew in a thick piece of thread that can be tied up to create the hanging loop.

Pine-cone angels

These angels are loads of fun for the kids to make. The basic idea is to use a pine cone as the angel's body and allow the kids to create wings, dresses and halos out of whatever you have available. You'll need to stick either a small ping-pong ball or a wooden or polystyrene ball that you can get in craft shops to the top to create the angel's head, and then get the kids to draw on the angel's features using felt-tip pens. Alternatively, you could also use a smaller pine cone or another seed object if you want to keep a natural look.

Holly, ivy and mistletoe

If you're lucky enough to live somewhere where there's an abundance of holly, ivy or mistletoe that can be gathered and used to craft some household decorations, there's a whole stack of pieces that you can make. I'd suggest gardening gloves to wear if you're working with holly. You can get the kids to wind branches around a stick to create a centrepiece to go on the table or mantelpiece, or get them to gather your finds into decorative bunches and tie them up with red ribbon to hang around the house. If you can get hold of some flower-arranging foam, you can get them to craft a table decoration using all the bits they've gathered, along with any other household additions such as baubles or streamers that they might like to include.

Twig stars

For this task you need to pick some flexible twigs, not dried ones you've found on the ground, as you need their natural malleability to bend them into shape. Get the kids to pick some suitable twigs and strip them of leaves. Next, bend two of your twigs into triangles without snapping them completely. Bind together the two ends of each stick with string and tie in place, then position your two triangles over the top of each other and carefully bind them together. Next, spray or paint the twigs gold and leave them to dry, before looping some string or ribbon around them so that they can be hung from the tree.

Other Christmas Decoration Ideas

If outside is looking a bit wet and windy, there are loads of Christmassy crafty bits you can make without having to tramp around in the stormy rain. Below are a few ideas.

Clay decorations

Making clay decorations is as easy as pie and allows kids to make things in whatever shape they fancy. Get some kids' clay from your local craft shop and roll out a slab per child. Get them to cut out the shape of the decoration they want to make using a fairly blunt knife. They might choose a star, a Christmas bell or tree, or even a stocking. Once it's cut out, pierce a string-sized hole at the top of the shape and pop them in the oven to bake or leave them out to dry, depending on the clay you're using. Once cooled down, this is where the fun part begins. Give the kids whatever you have for them to use to decorate their pendants and allow them to get stuck in – I won't point out all these, but do have a look for alternatives. They can roll their star in glue and glitter, wrap it in tin foil or paint on a design. Have a rummage among your crafty bits and encourage them to use whatever you have an abundance of. Finally, loop a piece of string through the hole and hang your decoration on the tree.

Tin-foil pendants

Kitchen foil is ideal for kids to use to craft some tree pendants. Give each child a sheet of foil, get them to fold it in half and glue the two duller sides together. Next, take a ballpoint pen and get the kids to gently draw their design on one of the sides (without pressing too hard, as you don't want the foil to rip). It can be anything Christmas-related, from a tree to Father Christmas's hat, or even a reindeer if they are good at drawing. Once done, turn it over and you'll see how it's given the decorations an embossed-type effect. Carefully cut around each of the designs and thread a piece of string through a hole on the top so they're ready to be hung from the tree. To make the pendant more sturdy, you can double up the tin foil and stick the two pieces on card to create a double-sided pendant.

Felt garlands and pendants

Felt has to be my favourite material to work with when doing creative stuff with kids. It comes in loads of bright colours, it can be stuck together and it cuts really easily so the kids can do the cutting out themselves. Get yourself a pile of multicoloured felt, some child-friendly scissors and glue. Ask the kids to sketch out the design they want to produce and then show them how to cut the shapes out of the felt. Encourage them to keep the shapes simple, such as trees and stars. They can then get stuck into cutting and sticking bits on before you finally string them together to create a felt garland or pass a piece of string through a hole at the top to create a Christmas-tree decoration.

The Hugginses' Present Pie

What's the game?

This is a really fun way to distribute presents to kids. My friends Nick and John used to do this with their kids every Christmas. They got fed up with little hands poking and prodding and ruining the surprise for Christmas Day. You need to make sure your presents are small enough to fit in your box and light enough to be pulled out on a piece of string.

What do I need to play it?

A big box, lots and lots of wrapping or brown paper, string, labels and presents that are small enough to fit in the box and light enough to be pulled out with string.

How many kids and what age?

As many kids as are with you for Christmas, though I'd avoid putting more than four presents in each box. Great for all ages as adults can give the younger kids a helping hand.

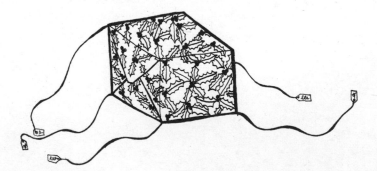

How do I play it?

- Wrap your presents up as normal, securely tie a long piece of string (about three metres) onto each of the gifts and tie a label to the end with the person's name on it.

- Place all the presents in a big cardboard box with the lid off. Then wrap the box so that it's entirely covered with paper, with holes at the four corners, and with one or two of the strings coming out of each hole with the labels attached to the end.

- Place the box under the tree.

- At the appointed present-opening time, get the kids to each take hold of the piece of string with their name on it and all pull simultaneously to release the presents from the box, so that they burst through the wrapping paper and into their laps.

Human Christmas Tree

What's the game?

This game will put the piles of ribbon, wrapping paper and other present packaging you have left at the end of the present opening to good use, adding an element of fun to clearing it all away.

What do I need to play it?

A big messy pile of post-present-opening debris.

How many kids and what age?

As many or as few as are sat around your tree and ideal for all ages.

How do I play it?

- Split into two teams, or three if there are quite a few of you. The ideal number to have in each team is three to four.

- Divide up all the leftover wrapping paper, ribbons and packaging equally so that there's a healthy pile for each team. You might want to top these up with extra Christmas decorations you have lying around.

- Decide who's going to be the Christmas tree in each team. Teams then have five minutes to turn their elected player into the best Christmas tree, using the leftover debris.

- Prizes awarded for creative use of materials as well as closeness to the traditional Christmas-tree form.

Father Christmas's Beard

What's the game?

Teams race to see who can create the best Father Christmas within a set period of time.

What do I need to play it?

Lots of cotton-wool balls and a pot of petroleum jelly per team. You will also need chairs and a stopwatch.

How many kids and what age?

At least four of you and as many others as want to play. With a helping hand for the younger kids, this one's ideal for all ages.

How do I play it?

- Get everyone into teams and ask the players to nominate who will be their Father Christmas.

- Father Christmas sits in the chair, with the other players surrounding him. Each team is given an equal share of cotton-wool balls and a pot of petroleum jelly.

- On the word 'Go!', teams race to create the most recognisable Father Christmas by sticking cotton-wool balls onto their nominated player's face using petroleum jelly.

- The best Father Christmas after sixty seconds wins.

Six

Fun for
All the Family

An afternoon of games with the family is undoubtedly my favourite type of organised fun. Games have a brilliant knack of bringing out people's true characters and personalities, so that those known for hiding their light under a bushel are given a moment to shine. Whether it's your Uncle Ted's mesmerising acting skills or a young cousin's artistic prowess, there should be something in this chapter to allow everyone their moment of glory.

Race on Your Face

What's the game?

This had us in stitches when we played it around the dinner table one Christmas Eve. It was the sight of various family members pulling fantastically funny faces that provided the most entertainment. It's not ideal for teaching your children table manners, but during one of those very long lunches where they have to stay in their seats it's a great way to keep them absorbed for a little bit longer.

What do I need to play it?

Something small and fairly flat, like one of those biscuits for cheese or an after-dinner mint per person.

How many family members?

Everyone that's around the dinner table.

How do I play it?

- Players lean their heads back and place the appointed item in the centre of their foreheads. You might need an umpire to make sure that all items are positioned in the same place, to prevent some players having an unfair advantage.

- On the word 'Go!', players race to get the item into their mouth by wrinkling and moving their face. If it falls off, the player has to place it back in the middle of their forehead and start again. First one to get the item in their mouth wins.

- There is a method to making this work, but if I tell you here it'll ruin the fun and give you an unfair advantage. Go figure it out!

Kate's Drawing Game

What's the game?

You might be fooled into thinking artistic types will have an advantage in this game, but their attention to aesthetics is in fact a hindrance. If you can hold a pencil, you can play this. Teams have to guess the word their team member is drawing. Brilliant for big boisterous family groups, but easily scaled down to however many of you there are.

What do I need to play it?

Some pens and paper.

How many family members?

Great with groups of all sizes and ages, but as with all these family games the younger kids might need a helping hand. You'll need one person to act as facilitator.

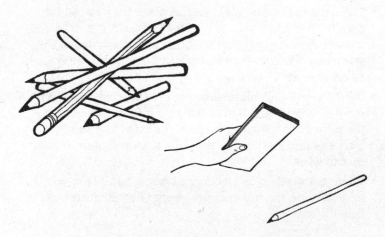

How do I play it?

- First of all, you need a list of subjects to draw. I'd suggest coming up with words around four themes, for example food, film, history, sport and so on. You can get as obscure or as personal as you like. A section on Granddad's bad habits might be interesting. As you write your list, you need to be sure that your words aren't too 'out there', or, more importantly, too hard to draw.

- Split everyone into two teams (or more if you're playing in a large group), send them off into separate rooms and position the facilitator somewhere in a room that's equidistant between them.

- On the word 'Go!', players on each team take it in turns to race out to the facilitator, each be given the same word and race back to draw it out for their team members, who have to guess what it is. Players mustn't speak (obviously), mime or write down the word. Only drawing is allowed. It's up to you whether players can draw an ear and give 'sounds like' clues.

- As soon as they guess correctly, another player races out to get the next word from the facilitator before racing back and drawing it.

- The first team to correctly identify all the words wins.

- If you're a little concerned about how trustworthy each player is, then I'd suggest having an umpire who sits in each room to ensure there's no cheating.

In the Manner of the Word

What's the game?

This is my mum's favourite game and one that is an obligatory part of the proceedings at every family Christmas. Being the mildly extrovert character that she is, I'm sure it has something to do with the fact that she's able to fling herself about; maybe it's evidence she missed her dramatic calling. Great for budding actors, it's easy to explain and just as easy to pick up – a winner for the whole family. It involves a team member carrying out a designated action in the manner of a particular adverb, while the rest of the team have to decide what the adverb is.

What do I need to play it?

Nothing.

How many family members?

Ideal for groups of four to ten and easy for kids over six to pick up.

How do I play it?

- Decide who's first to go, get them to step out of the room and close the door to ensure they're well out of earshot.

- Meanwhile, the rest of the players whisper together to decide which adverb they'd like to play out on this round. If you're playing with young kids, try something simple such as 'grumpily' or 'hungrily'. Make sure you choose an adverb that the player outside the room will understand, but equally one that's challenging enough for them not to guess straightaway.

- Once decided, the player is called back in. They must then choose someone and ask them to do something 'in the manner of the word'. For example, if the word was 'regally' and the selected player was asked to bake a cake in the manner of the word, they might choose to smatter their cake-baking performance with a few royal waves, or ensure they take off and polish their crown before rolling up their royal sleeves to ice the cake.

- As soon as the player has guessed the correct adverb, they swap with whoever's performance helped them guess, and it's that person's turn to go out of the room.

Personalities

What's the game?

This is a favourite of many families I know. It appeals to all ages and gets everyone moving around, preventing anyone falling into a post-feast coma. The game involves players choosing a character and then in teams trying to guess who each other is. The ultimate aim is to make the other players join your family team.

What do I need to play it?

Paper and pens.

How many family members?

Great for big groups of all ages. Can't be played with any fewer than eight.

How do I play it?

- The objective of the game is to guess the personalities that other players have given themselves.

- Nominate one game leader and then divide into teams of between three and five, depending on how many people are playing. Get each team to position themselves in different corners of the room.

- Next, everyone decides on a character without telling anyone else, and they scribble it down on a slip of paper (it could be Charlie Chaplin, Tom Cruise, the Queen or David Beckham, for example). Give the names to the game leader, who puts them in a hat. It's important that players choose characters they know everyone will know, and they should also think of avoiding a personality that's too obviously like themselves. The idea is to fox other players so that they cannot guess who you are.

- Once the names are collected, the game leader reads the full list aloud twice. If you want to be strict about it, you can make this once. All players must attempt to memorise the names.

- The aim of the game is to guess who chose which personality, with the winner being the person who is the last to be identified.

- The first team tries to correctly guess the character of someone on the opposite team. To do this you should try and think what sort of character that person might choose to be. For example, if your aunt has a Beatrix Potter fetish, you might conclude that she's Jemima Puddle-Duck – unless you think someone else has chosen it as a red herring.

- If a team makes a correct guess, the player they have identified moves over to join their group. Because they made a correct guess, the same team carries on guessing the other players' identities with correctly identified individuals moving over to join them, until they get one wrong. It then moves to the next team to take up the challenge.

- If the other team have been listening carefully, they will have memorised the identities of all the players that were called over and will then call them back to their group. Then they should hopefully add a couple more as they guess the names of those who haven't yet been identified.

- The game plays on in this way until there is one big team of everybody bar one. The winner is the last person left who hasn't been identified.

Theatrical Chinese Whispers

What's the game?

This game was invented by my siblings and cousins after we had bored our parents rigid with incessant demands to play Chinese Whispers at our dinner table. By bending the rules slightly, we liberated ourselves from our seats.

What do I need to play it?

Hardly anything, but if you want to go to town you can bring in all sorts of props.

How many family members?

You need more than three of you to make it work. The younger kids might need a helping hand.

How do I play it?

- Everyone splits into two teams.
- Team A goes out of the room and Team B thinks of an action or sequence of actions – as mundane or as dramatic as you choose, for example pruning the roses or winning the Grand National.
- One member of Team A returns into the room. The action is acted out in front of them by a member of Team B.
- Another member of Team A then enters the room.
- The first member of Team A then needs to act out their interpretation of what they've seen to their team member.
- And so the sequence goes on, until the last team member enters the room, sees the sequence acted out and has to guess what the performance is about.
- The game then plays on, with the other team going out.

Kim's Memory Game

What's the game?

I used to love this game as a kid. It's a memory game that involves memorising all the items on a tray within a specified period of time.

What do I need to play it?

A tray, a tea towel that's big enough to cover it and a collection of twenty small items, such as a watch, a cotton reel, an apple – you get the idea. You'll also need some paper and pens.

How many family members?

This is great for all ages and all group sizes.

How do I play it?

- Secretly prepare a tray of twenty small items and cover it over with the tea towel.

- Next, get everyone to split into teams, making sure that children are partnered with adults, and give each team a paper and pen. Make sure they're sat where they can all see the covered tray placed in the middle.

- When you're ready, explain that the tea towel is going to be lifted and everyone has forty-five seconds to remember all the items on the tray. They need to remember them and not write them down. When the forty-five seconds is up, cover the tray again and get each of the teams to write down as many of the items as they can recall.

- The team that remembers the most items wins.

Flight Commander Colonel Warrington Smyth

What's the game?

This is a great memory game that's ideal to play around the dinner table at big family gatherings when all the eating is done. It involves players trying to remember a routine of actions performed and added to by each guest as they take their turn to make a toast.

What do I need to play it?

Players with full bellies and full glasses.

How many family members?

Great for all ages and as many as are sat around your table.

How do I play it?

- The game involves players taking it in turns to make a toast and acting out a routine of actions that each player then adds to as their turn comes around.

- The person to begin the game briefly explains the rules and announces, 'I'd like to make a toast to Flight Commander Colonel Warrington Smyth.' After the toast is made, the player takes a sip of their drink and performs an action such as tapping their glass, knocking on the table or even doing a pirouette, before sitting down again.

- It's then the turn of the next player along. This player stands up, makes the toast, takes a sip of their drink, performs the action the last player did and then adds their own.

- The game continues around and around the table. If a player forgets a move, they are out.

- The last player who manages to remember the entire routine is declared the winner.

The Cereal-Packet Game

What's the game?

This game will appeal to yoga-lovers as it allows guests to a demonstrate their dexterity and balance. It's brilliant to watch and you might be surprised by the suppleness of some people in your group. The aim of the game is to demonstrate flexibility by bending down and picking up a cereal packet using only the teeth as it gets cut down lower and lower.

What do I need to play it?

An empty cereal packet.

How many family members?

As many as want to play it. Kids should be aged six and over.

How do I play it?

- Get everybody to stand in a circle and place a cereal packet in the middle. Each player takes it in turns to step forward, bend down and retrieve the packet with their teeth. The rules are that no body part other than the player's feet is allowed to touch the floor, and no other object must be used to give them balance.

- If players fail after two goes, they're out. If you want to be strict about it, you can make it one go.

- Once the remaining players have completed the task, you then need to trim the top layer off the cereal packet by about five centimetres. You then go around the circle again, with each player attempting to pick it up with their teeth within two goes.

- The game plays on, with the packet getting lower and lower as more of it is trimmed off at the end of each round, and more and more players drop out, until the last man standing is declared the winner.

Dough You Know What It Is?

What's the game?

If you're bored of the classic game of Charades and fancy something a little different, this one's a great alternative and, to my mind, a whole lot more amusing. Some friends and their kids came and stayed with us one weekend, and the kids brought along their play dough, a soft, clay-like substance that doesn't go hard when you make shapes out of it. We were taking it in turns to demonstrate our sculpting ability when it occurred to us that there was a brilliant game in this.

What do I need to play it?

Ideally, you need a different-coloured dough for each team. If you're struggling to get your hands on play dough, you can make some salt dough, which works in the same way. Simply mix together three cups of flour, one cup of salt, four cups of water and one tablespoon of glycerine (available from chemists or supermarkets). You can then add food colouring so that each team has a different colour.

The easy alternative is to use a reusable adhesive putty. You'll also need some pens and paper and a hat or bowl to put the slips of paper into.

How many family members?

Works for a small to medium-sized group of between four and twelve. Kids really need to be seven and over to properly grasp how to play.

How do I play it?

- The object of the game is to be the first team to communicate a word through sculpting it out of dough for their teammates to guess.

- To start off, you need to get one person to write out twenty things for each of the players in the game. Make sure that all the suggestions can feasibly be sculpted out of dough. Put these in a hat or bowl in the middle of the table.

- Next, get yourselves into teams. The ideal number in each team is three, but as long as there is more than one, you can make it work.

- Everyone takes it in turns to be the sculptor for the team. Decide who's going first. That person pulls a slip of paper out of the hat, looks at it and then passes it on to the player in another team whose turn it is to sculpt.

- On the word 'Go!', the sculptor in each team simultaneously starts squeezing, crafting and shaping their dough to somehow communicate what the word is. It's up to you whether you allow animation of the dough – animating the bird so it flies through the sky by waving it around in the air, for example.

- The very clear rule, however, is that communication must be through the dough model and any other sort of body action is not allowed.

- The first team to guess correctly wins a point. The first team to ten points wins.

Call My Bluff

What's the game?

If some of the earlier games are too wacky for you and your family, Call My Bluff is a more relaxed and generally more civilised option that's particularly good for older kids. The game requires players to draft a plausible fake dictionary definition, so any youngsters at the table might need a helping hand.

What do I need to play it?

A dictionary, paper and pens.

How many family members?

At least three of you, aged eight and upwards.

How do I play it?

- Players take it in turns to lead each round. Each leader chooses an obscure word from the dictionary, one which they're fairly certain no one knows the definition of.

- All the guests need to write a plausible definition for the word. The objective of the game is to confuse other players into selecting yours as the correct one. If you have an inkling of what the actual definition is, write this out as if correct. It'll earn you extra points.

- When the definitions are ready, everyone secretly submits them to the holder of the dictionary. The dictionary holder needs to write out the actual definition on another slip of paper to prevent players easily guessing the correct one.

- Each definition is then read out and players must guess which is the right one. Scoring is as follows:
  - All players choosing the actual definition get two points.
  - Players also get a point for each person who selects the definition they wrote.
  - If no one identifies the correct definition, the leader of that round gets a point.
  - If someone has written a definition that is close to the real one, that person also gets two points.
- The game then moves on with different people leading each round. Once everyone has had a go, the player with the highest score wins.
- N.B. It's hugely important that everyone writes as clearly as possible, because if a player can't read someone else's writing when it's their turn to read out the definition, they're likely to give away the fact that it's not the actual one.

You Have a Face

What's the game?

If you're proud of your extensive vocabulary and take pleasure in showing it off, this game is for you. It's a test of your knowledge of adjectives. If you run out of words, you're out.

What do I need to play it?

A sound knowledge of the alphabet and a decent grasp of vocabulary.

How many family members?

As many as are seated around the table.

How do I play it?

- To get started, the group collectively nominates a letter.
- The first person to go then remarks to their neighbour, 'You have a face!' The neighbour enquires, 'What kind of a face?' And the first player replies using an adjective beginning with the chosen letter. So if the nominated letter is 'A' then 'An amphibian face' would be a suitable response.
- The owner of the amphibian face then says to their neighbour, 'You have a face!' and the game goes around, knocking out players who can't think of a word beginning with that letter.

Wink Murder

What's the game?

A game of little effort involving death by winking.

What do I need to play it?

Paper and a pen.

How many family members?

More than three but hard to play with over twenty. Suitable for all ages.

How do I play it?

- First, write out a slip of paper for every player, ensuring you have one M for 'murderer' and a D for 'detective', with the rest of the slips featuring a V for 'victim'.
- Put all the slips in a hat and get everyone to pick one out.
- If you're the detective, your objective is to spot the killer; if you're the murderer, it's to kill everyone by the evil wink of your eye; and if you're a victim, you die a blood-curdling death as soon as someone winks at you.
- The game ends when the detective spots who the murderer is. Repeat the game with the roles swapped around.
- The winner is the detective who manages to spot the murderer with the smallest number of victims.

Up Jenkins

What's the game?

Up Jenkins is a very simple Victorian game of detection that works brilliantly after dinner. It's ideal to decide who's going to do the washing-up, as the forfeit for the losing team is banishment to the kitchen sink while the winners kick back and enjoy another game.

What do I need to play it?

A coin.

How many family members?

A nice full table – the more the merrier. Suitable for all the family.

How do I play it?

- Split the table into two teams of members sitting next to each other. The first team takes the coin and secretly passes it between themselves under the table, minimising movements or laying false movement clues as to the whereabouts of the coin.

- When someone on the opposing team knows where the coin is, they shout 'Up Jenkins!' and point at the offending player, who then must stand up and reveal whether the coin is in their fist. If correct, the guessing team scores a point. The coin is then handed over for the other team to pass around.

- First team to five wins the pleasure of not doing the washing-up.

Duck Roulette

What's the game?

The flotilla of feathered friends who share our stretch of the Thames all have names. There are Marvin and Amanda the mandarins, James and Arcadia the white swans and Jerry and Terry the gay mallards who hang out in the bush in our garden.

My boyfriend Barney and our friend Ollie came up with this to provide a focus to the regular duck-feeding frenzy that happens in front of our boat each morning.

What do I need to play it?

Some ducks, geese or swans. You need at least ten of them to make it a decent game.

How many kids?

A child could play it on their own but having a friend with them makes it much more fun.

How do I play it?

- This game is best played with a large group of ducks.

- The objective of the game is to successfully feed the duck you pick out from the group.

- First of all, pick your duck. You must now throw your duck-food item to the duck that you've named.

- If your nominated duck eats your piece of bread, you get a point.

Seven

Classic
Fun for *Kids*

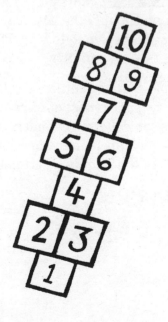

There has been a tradition of playing games at children's parties for centuries, and for generations they have followed a much-loved formula. From the arrival of the children with their nervous smiles to the party bag on departure, there's a ritual to be adhered to. The same can also be said of the game-playing spectacle that ensues. It's a way for parents to relive their cherished childhood memories and pass them on for their children to share.

Nostalgia aside, the classic games are also classics for a reason: they are simply brilliant games and their brilliance makes them as much fun for adults as for kids. Musical Chairs played at a New Year's Eve party is undeniably the best way to move things on from a sedate evening to a festival of feel-good anarchy.

The following chapter features a collection of those classic party games most of us cut our milk teeth on. Here are some warm reminders as well as some fresh inspiration to ensure your young friends will be thoroughly entertained.

Conkers

What's the game?

Conkers has been a playground favourite for centuries and continues to be the autumn game of choice for schoolchildren across the UK. A 2008 poll in the *Daily Telegraph* of 2,000 schoolchildren named it as their number-one favourite.

Although a British invention, the game has since gone international. From Canada to France, wherever the horse chestnut prospers schoolchildren can be found hanging the shiny seeds on string and smashing their mates' ones to pieces. Its popularity has grown to such an extent that a world championship is held each year in Northamptonshire. The French, who make themselves a regular feature at the event, claim to have a strong strategy behind their game. In a recent newspaper article the French Federation's chairman Stephane Jally stated, 'Conkers is like rugby. The British invented it, but we do it better.'

There's a pub along the river from where we live that always has conker accoutrements on the bar come the fresh winds of autumn. We spent most Saturdays last September chugging down the river to plonk ourselves on our favourite bar stools and challenge the locals to a game.

Although tempting to come up with a variation, some classics shouldn't be messed with.

What do I need to play it?

Conkers, string, a skewer or drill, and scissors.

How many kids and what age?

A minimum of two, though a tournament is a great way to fill an afternoon with a bunch of kids. Players should be aged seven and over.

How do I play it?

- First up, get the kids to select their conkers on the basis of form, symmetry and lack of cracks.

- Next, prepare for battle. Drill a hole down the middle using a sharp skewer (adults should do this part). If drilled badly you can weaken the strength of the conker. Try to drill or skewer as straight as possible. Avoid the lighter-coloured circle on top as it's not as waxy as the rest of the skin and therefore more likely to crack.

- Thread a piece of string through the hole. You need one that's about 25 centimetres in length. Once you've threaded your string through, tie multiple knots at the bottom to ensure it doesn't fall off. You should also tie a knot at the point the string comes out of the top of the conker. This prevents it sliding up the string and maximises its force when in play.

- Once conkers are threaded and contestants are ready to play, two players face each other with their conkers hanging down on the string and the string wrapped around their hands a couple of times for extra support.

- Players then take it in turns to thwack and hopefully crack their opponent's conker, by stretching the string taut with the hitting conker drawn up towards them, and then using the length of string to target the full force towards the opponent's hanging conker on its release.

Make Your Own Fun

- If a player misses, they are allowed two extra goes.
- If the strings tangle, the first player to call, 'Strings!' gets an extra shot.
- If a player strikes and causes their opponent's conker to spin in a full circle, the player gets another go.
- If a player drops their conker or it's knocked out of their hand, the other player can shout, 'Stamps!' and then is able to jump on it, hopefully to crack it. If the first player cries, 'No stamps!' first, then the other player is not allowed to stamp on it.
- The winner is the one whose conker lasts the longest. Each time a conker defeats another it clocks up its victim's numbers. In a contest of two new conkers the winner's conker thus becomes 'a one-er' (bring back memories?). If the same conker beats another successful conker who was, say, 'a fourer', the winning conker then goes on to take on its defeated conker's score – making it 'a fiver'.
- Now, when I was younger there was a whole lot of jiggery-pokery around how to make your conkers as un-crackable as possible, from soaking them in vinegar to baking them in the oven. I'm not sure how effective any of these are. I remember being convinced that doing both was the secret behind my 'elevener' at school. One tip I recently heard which does make a lot of sense is: if you put a selection of conkers in water and some of them float, discard these ones and use the heavier and denser ones at the bottom of the bowl as they're likely to be stronger.

Oranges and Lemons

What's the game?

'Oranges and Lemons' is a nursery rhyme dating back several centuries which evolved into a popular children's game. The rhyme sings of many of the churches of London, and its melody is said to match the sound of the different bells across the city.

The sinister end to the game involves pretending to chop off each other's heads. It's believed children added this part of the rhyme some time in the late eighteenth century. The song refers to the execution of prisoners, many of whom were imprisoned for debt, hence the line, 'When will you pay me?' The unfortunate prisoner would be informed of his impending death by a gallows man carrying a candle towards his cell ('Here comes a candle to light you to bed') before the dark last line: 'And here comes a chopper to chop off your head!' A charming child's verse.

What do I need to play it?

Some willing children.

How many kids and what age?

You need at least six kids to make it work, though a roomful is much better. This one is great for kids over five.

How do I play it?

- To start, get your children into pairs and standing in a line. The first pair steps forward to form an arch by raising their hands up and clasping hold of their partner's hands in front of them.

- Players then file in pairs through the arch while everyone sings the words of the well-known nursery rhyme:

  'Oranges and lemons,' say the bells of St Clement's.
  'You owe me five farthings,' say the bells of St Martin's.
  'When will you pay me?' say the bells of Old Bailey.
  'When I grow rich,' say the bells of Shoreditch.
  'When will that be?' say the bells of Stepney.
  'I do not know,' says the great bell of Bow.
  Here comes a candle to light you to bed,
  And here comes a chopper to chop off your head!

- The pairs peel back and file through the arch again until on the last word the children forming the arch drop their arms to catch the pair of children who are passing through at that point.

- When caught, these children are then out and must form another arch next to the existing one to create a steadily lengthening tunnel, through which the children have to run faster and faster to escape the chopper.

- Some people also play a version in which the children chop down their arms all the way through the last line of the verse – it's up to you which variation you think works best.

Blind Man's Buff

What's the game?

Blind Man's Buff can be traced back to the Tudor period.
There are some historical records showing it to be a popular
pastime among Henry VIII's courtiers, and its popularity was
reinforced during the hearty parlour-game afternoons of the
Victorian era.

There's some confusion as to whether it's called Blind
Man's 'Bluff' or 'Buff'. The British will generally choose the
'buff' variant, which is in fact nothing to do with nudity and
is an old-fashioned word for a gentle push. The Americans
call it 'bluff', which might be as a result of poor transatlantic
carriage, or it may relate to the fact that 'bluff' is an old term
for being blindfolded.

Call it what you choose, the game is yet another variant
of It and remains a great way to entertain the kids as well as
the adults on a rainy afternoon.

What do I need to play it?

A blindfold and a confined space to play in, such as a garden
or room.

How many kids and what age?

At least five of you to make it a decent game. It works best
with children aged seven and over.

How do I play it?

- Choose who's going to be 'it' first and put a blindfold on them.
- The rest of the players must then run away, but they cannot leave the confines of the space.
- The blindfolded player then has to try to catch the others, who run around taunting him or her.
- Now, at this point there are three variants that you can choose to play:
    1. When a player is caught, they're out and have to sit at the side.
    2. The caught person becomes the blindfolded player.
    3. Or the Victorians' favourite: the blindfolded player has to guess who the caught person is by feeling their face and body – our stiff-upper-lipped forebears were quite racy really!

Hopscotch

What's the game?

Hopscotch can be dated back to the Roman Empire, when soldiers used the game to improve their footwork and agility in preparation for battle. The game continues to be played all over the world and has spawned many variants. I've featured the version most commonly practised in school playgrounds today.

What do I need to play it?

Some chalk, something to use as a marker and some pavement or tarmac to play on.

How many kids and what age?

Great to play on your own or in a small gang, and perfect for kids aged six and upwards.

How do I play it?

- To play this classic game, begin by chalking out your play area as shown opposite.

- The first player takes their marker (it can be a stone or a coin, for example) and tosses it onto square number one.

- The hopper then has to hop and jump up the course, missing out the square that the marker landed on. They must land on one leg when it's a single square, or straddle both squares if it's a double.

- Once completed, they must then turn around and hop back, picking up their marker on the way, before throwing it onto the number-two square and repeating the process.

Make Your Own Fun

- If the player falls over, misses a square or steps on a line, their go ends and it's the turn of the next player.
- Players always begin their turn where they last left off. The first player to complete the course working through all the numbers wins the game.

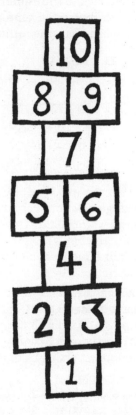

Stocking Balls

What's the game?

This game involves bouncing a tennis ball that sits in the toe of a stocking on a wall behind in time to a rhyme. It was a real fad at our school and I became rather good at it.

What do I need to play it?

A tennis ball and a stocking per player, and a hard wall to bounce off.

How many kids and what age?

Great for kids to play on their own or in a small group. I'd recommend it for those aged six and upwards.

How do I play it?

* Put a ball in a stocking and get the child to stand with their back against the wall, holding the opposite end of the stocking to where the ball's hanging. They might want to wind it around their hand a couple of times to ensure it's secure.

* Now bounce the ball on the wall behind by swinging the stocking so that it bounces above right of the right shoulder, then swing it around so it bounces above left of the left shoulder. Then swing it down so that it bounces between the legs before reversing back through this sequence.

* The elasticity of the stocking and the velocity of the movement will create a rhythmic feel that, once mastered, will have the child bouncing away for hours.

* Practise this until the three-bounce sequence can be executed without thinking too much.

* Now practise doing a double bounce to either side.

Make Your Own Fun

- Now practise alternating these movements. Once this can be done with ease, the child is ready to bounce in time to the following rhyme:

  Have a lollipop, Sir?
  No, Sir.
  Why, Sir?
  Because I've got a cold, Sir.
  Where did you get your cold, Sir?
  At the North Pole, Sir.
  What were you doing there, Sir?
  Catching polar bears, Sir.
  How many did you catch, Sir?
  One, two, three, Sir.
  The rest caught me, Sir.
  Threw me in the sea, Sir.
  That's the end of me, Sir.

- The child needs to bounce the ball using the three-bounce sequence all the way through until they get to the counting line, 'One, two, three, Sir,' where they do a double bounce before returning to the three-bounce sequence again.

French Skipping

What's the game?

This was another school-playground top-ten game when I was young. My two best friends, Leah and Adele, and I played it endlessly until it was banished from the playground when we caused a rather nasty tripping accident. With such incidents in mind, this game does come with a word of warning about ensuring children aren't running around in the vicinity while the game's being played.

What do I need to play it?

A two-and-a-half-metre-long piece of thick elastic with the two ends tied together to create a big loop.

How many kids and what age?

We picked it up when we were around seven or eight. You need a minimum of three kids to play it, or a few more if they don't mind a bit of waiting around.

How do I play it?

- Get two of the kids to face each other about two metres apart, and get them to step into the elastic, stretching it out with their ankles, with the third child standing in the middle.
- The jumping child then starts with their left foot inside the elastic loop and right foot just outside it, and then jumps over to the other side, so the right foot is inside the loop and the left foot is outside.

- You repeat this sequence in time to a rhyme, and on the last word of the rhyme you jump and land with your feet on each side of the elastic loop. Here are some classic French Skipping rhymes:

    Chocolate cake, when you bake,
    How many minutes will you take?
    One, two, three, four.

    England, Ireland, Scotland, Wales,
    Inside, outside, inside, on!

    Old Mrs Mason broke her basin,
    On the way to London Station.
    How much did it cost?
    One, two, three, four.

    Charlie Chaplin sat on a pin,
    How many inches did it go in?
    One, two, three, four.

- The kids will need to play around with the rhymes and decide on an agreed sequence. If the player gets the routine wrong, they have to stop and swap to let another player have a turn.

- If a player successfully gets through the whole sequence, the elastic is then raised to the knees, fondly known as 'kneesies', and then the thighs – 'thighsies'.

What's the Time, Mr Wolf?

What's the game?

This is a classic children's party game. I can remember playing it for the first time: it must have been Easter or some other day of religious celebration as I can recollect the tedium of Sunday school being replaced by an afternoon of games. I can still see the heavily patterned rug beneath my feet and hear the muffled ticking of the grandfather clock as we stepped towards our imminent deaths.

What do I need to play it?

Nothing at all.

How many kids and what age?

At least three, though it's great to play with a large group. Ideal for kids aged four and upwards.

How do I play it?

- Decide which child is going to be Mr Wolf and stand them facing the wall, with the other children in a line about three metres behind them.

- The children then all simultaneously say 'What's the time, Mr Wolf?'

- Mr Wolf chooses a time and says 'It's X o'clock'. The children then all step forward however many paces o'clock it is: twelve for 12 o'clock, and so on. The tension begins to ratchet up as the children get nearer to Mr Wolf – especially if Mr Wolf pretends to be very unconcerned.

- This goes on until Mr Wolf decides they've had enough. The next time the children ask 'What's the time, Mr Wolf?', Mr Wolf shouts, 'Dinner time!' and then turns around and chases the squealing children until one is caught, whose turn it then is to become Mr Wolf.

Squeak Piggy Squeak

What's the game?

This is another parlour game favoured by those hyperactive young Victorians. It involves dizzily stumbling around and sitting on people's laps. It only really works if the kids know each other fairly well, as they need to guess whose lap they're sitting on.

What do I need to play it?

A blindfold.

How many kids and what age?

You need at least six children aged five and upwards. This is another one that's great to play with large groups.

How do I play it?

- Get your group to sit in a circle, blindfold whoever's going to go first and get them to stand in the middle.

- Someone then needs to turn the blindfolded child at least three times to make sure they're disorientated and dizzy.

- The child then has to fumble around to find one of the children sat in the circle. They sit on a child's lap and say, 'Squeak piggy squeak,' at which point the child whose lap the player is sitting on lets out a squeak.

- The blindfolded player has to guess who it is. If they get it wrong, they have to carry on playing. If they get it right, it's the squeaking player's turn to be blindfolded.

Sardines

What's the game?

This game is a fun take on It, in which children hunt out and join the person who's 'it' until all players end up stuffed in the cupboard or under the bed.

What do I need to play it?

Some good-sized hiding places.

How many kids and what age?

Unless you have the sort of endless wardrobe found in *The Lion, the Witch and the Wardrobe*, this one's better played with small groups of, say, between three and six. Perfect for kids aged five and upwards.

How do I play it?

- Choose who's going to be 'it' first.

- That child runs off to hide while the others count to fifty.

- Depending on their age, you might need to help the hiding child to select a hiding place that's big enough to hold the number of children who are playing.

- Once the hiding child is safely hidden, the rest run to find him or her.

- As each child finds the hider, they join them in their hiding place until there is only one child left doing the hunting, and it's then their turn to be 'it'.

Eight

Competitive
Fun

Some kids are born competitive. They're the ones you'll find arm-wrestling their teddies in their cots or challenging other pram riders to a race. Most, however, locate their competitive spirit around the ages of five or six. It's the period when they become more aware of themselves and start to measure their own capabilities against those of their peers.

But it's not always the kids themselves who are to blame when a true contest-obsessive is created. In many cases, it's the parent who nurtures this cut-throat mindset in their child. You've probably come across them: they're usually found screaming on the sidelines of kids' football matches or accidentally tripping up a rival to make sure little Lola wins the ballet competition.

Extremists aside, injecting an element of competitive spirit into an afternoon of children's fun will have your young friends raring to get involved.

Balloon Race

What's the game?

Children find these giddy antics great fun and the images the game delivers will certainly add colour to your summer photo album.

What do I need to play it?

A balloon per racer.

How many kids and what age?

As many as will fit on the starting line. Great for kids aged seven and upwards.

How do I play it?

- Get the kids lined up on the starting line, each with a balloon in hand.

- On the word 'Go!', the children race to the finishing line, batting their balloon in front of them with one hand to keep it in the air.

- If the balloon touches the floor or the child holds rather than bats it, then they have to go back to the starting line.

- First across the finishing line wins.

Hula-Hoop Relay

What's the game?

The art of playing with a hoop has engaged children for centuries. The original whipping hoop was a cane hoop that children used to chase down the street with a stick. The 1950s saw a reinvention of the classic hoop by Wham-O-Toys and in 1957 the world witnessed the birth of the Hula Hoop. This game is an adaptation of the classic relay race, but with the improvisation of a Hula Hoop being passed down the line.

What do I need to play it?

A Hula Hoop.

How many kids and what age?

Enough for two teams to make it a race. Kids need to be old enough to wiggle a Hula Hoop around their waists.

How do I play it?

- Get into two teams and spread out parallel to each other in two lines.
- The person at the top of the line starts by completing three successful spins of the hoop before passing it down the line for the next person to do the same, and so on.
- First team to finish wins.

Flowerpot Race

What's the game?

This is harder to explain than it is to play. It's a race to the finishing line using two flowerpot stepping stones that you move forward on. Confused? Read on.

What do I need to play it?

Two terracotta flowerpots per contestant, or old paint tins make a great alternative. They need to be strong enough to stand on.

How many kids and what age?

Enough kids to make it a race. Best for kids with a strong sense of balance, i.e. those aged seven and upwards.

How do I play it?

- Mark out a starting and finishing line. If you're particularly organised, you can mark out a more elaborate course around the garden.

- Contestants turn their flowerpots upside down and use them as stepping stones to race to the finishing line. Each contestant begins by standing on one flowerpot behind the starting line. When the race begins, they each place their second flowerpot in front of them and step onto it with both feet, before moving their first flowerpot in front and stepping onto that, and so on.

- The first person to reach the finishing line wins. If you fall off or touch the ground at all, you have to go back to the beginning and start all over again.

Slow Bicycle Race

What's the game?

This is a bicycle race around a designated course which contestants must complete without touching the ground. The *last* one across the finishing line wins, which means you have to do it as slowly as possible. If you put your foot on the ground or fall off, you're out.

Over and Under

What's the game?

This is a simple relay race involving children passing a balloon over their heads and between their legs.

What do I need to play it?

Two balloons.

How many kids and what age?

Ideally you need at least eight children to make two teams of four. This one works for kids aged six and over.

How do I play it?

- Get your gang to split into two teams and form two straight lines in front of you.
- Give each child at the front of the line a balloon.
- On the word 'Go!', the children have to alternately pass the balloon over their heads and between their legs.
- When the balloon gets to the last person, they have to run with it to the front of the line and begin again. This continues until the person who started is back at the front.
- Whichever team completes the task first wins.

Potato Race

What's the game?

Another one that's highly amusing to watch. As the kids are blindfolded, you do need to make sure they don't get too eager with their potato foraging and smack into each other.

What do I need to play it?

A blindfold and bucket per pair, and a sack of potatoes. You probably need around eight potatoes per player. If you want to prevent the kids getting mucky, give the potatoes a quick scrub first to get all the mud off and dry them out.

How many kids and what age?

Great for smaller groups, but you really need an even number. Four or six is perfect. This one works for younger kids as well.

How do I play it?

- Set up your course by scattering the potatoes in front of the competitors.
- Next, get the kids to pair up and put a blindfold on one of each of the pairs.
- On the word 'Go!', the blindfolded child must race around to grab as many potatoes as they can while their partner shouts out directions. When their arms are full, they race to their bucket and drop in their haul before returning to collect more.
- Once all the potatoes are collected, the pair with the most in their bucket wins.
- Play this twice so that everyone gets a turn to be blindfolded.

Egg-and-Spoon Race

What's the game?

An old favourite from school sports days. Players each race to the finishing line balancing an egg on a spoon.

What do I need to play it?

An egg and spoon per player and a clear space to hold a race.

How many kids and what age?

Enough kids to make it a race.

How do I play it?

- Get racers lined up at the starting line with their eggs (boiled or not, depending on how much mess you want to make, or use potatoes instead) balanced on their spoons.

- On the word 'Go!', contestants race to the finishing line. If their egg falls off the spoon, they must go back to the starting line and begin again. If their egg breaks, they are out.

- First across the line is the winner.

Blindfolded Ankle Race

What's the game?

A normal blindfolded race is made more complicated when contestants hold their ankles as they race towards the finishing line.

What do I need to play it?

A blindfold per player and enough room to have a race.

How many kids and what age?

Great for kids of walking age, and you need enough of them to make it a race.

How do I play it?

- Get contestants blindfolded and lined up at the starting line, bent over so they're holding their ankles. Racers have the option to adopt a forward-facing or backward-facing approach.

- On the word 'Go!', contestants attempt to race towards where they think the finishing line is while maintaining a hold on their ankles. You'll need a judge to shout 'Stop!' when the first three are across the finishing line and to redirect anyone who's heading for the garden pond.

- If holding their ankles makes the kids feel too dizzy, you can change the format to a blindfolded backwards running race.

Balloon Relay Race

What's the game?

This game is great to play indoors in a big room or outside in a sunny garden. Players form teams and race against each other while flapping a balloon with a newspaper towards their teammate.

What do I need to play it?

A balloon and newspaper per team.

How many kids and what age?

Great for kids of all ages. You'll need enough of them to make it a race.

How do I play it?

- Get contestants into teams; I'd recommend no more than six people in each one. Split each team up so that half are at one end of the track and half at the other.

- The first child in each team to race holds the newspaper and balloon in front of them.

- On the word 'Go!', they must flap the newspaper to create a draught that drives the balloon towards their teammate at the other end of the track. They must not hit the balloon with the newspaper. As balloons are full of air, they have a tendency to veer off course; it's harder than you might imagine it to be.

- As soon as they get their balloon to where their team member is standing, the newspaper is handed over and the next person continues the race by driving the balloon back to the other end of the track.

- The first team to complete the course wins.

Crab-Scuttle Relay

What's the game?

You know how crabs scuttle along the sand sideways? In this race, contestants do exactly that.

What do I need to play it?

Somewhere to race.

How many kids and what age?

A racing gang of strong children aged eight and upwards.

How do I play it?

- Get the kids to lie on their backs with their knees bent and hands and feet resting on the floor and get them to push themselves up to create the shape of a crab. Make sure they don't reach their arms over their heads to form a bridge, as this will put too much strain on their young arms and backs.

- Get everyone positioned at the starting line in a sideways position. On the word 'Go!', the crabs scuttle to the finishing line.

Wheelbarrow Relay

What's the game?

This is another village-fête classic.

What do I need to play it?

Some strong kids who are up for a race.

How many kids and what age?

A big group of kids who are old and strong enough to make this work. Ages eight and upwards only.

How do I play it?

- Mark out your racetrack. I'd suggest no more than seventy-five metres, otherwise your contestants will collapse before the race is over.

- Get everyone into pairs and then they can argue over who's going to be the wheelbarrow.

- Once that's agreed, get them all lined up at the starting line with the runner holding the wheelbarrow's ankles so that they're walking along on their hands.

- On the word 'Go!', players race to the finishing line. First across wins. Dropped wheelbarrows have to go back and start again.

100-Metre Roly Poly

What's the game?

This is quite simply a 100-metre race of continuous forward rolls. Neck strain is a potential hazard; reduce race length to 50 metres if you're concerned.

Water Bucket Race

What's the game?

This is an ideal game for a blazing-hot summer's afternoon. Kids race to transfer the water from one bucket to another using only a cup.

What do I need to play it?

Two buckets (one empty and one filled with water) and a cup per child, and somewhere to race.

How many kids and what age?

This is a race that works for small groups; you can even play it as a timed trial for one child. Suitable for all ages.

How do I play it?

- Set your two buckets at a reasonable distance apart. On the word 'Go!', kids have to transfer the water from one bucket to the other, one cup at a time, spilling as little as possible.

Fancy-Dress Relay

What's the game?

This is a very amusing race that uses clothes instead of a traditional relay baton.

What do I need to play it?

You need a set of clothes for each team. Each set should feature similar items to prevent any unfair advantages.

How many kids and what age?

Great for large or small groups. As long as a child can walk, they can play.

How do I play it?

- Get the teams lined up at the starting line with a set of clothes in front of whoever is racing first.

- On the word 'Go!', the first contestant has to put on the whole outfit over their own clothes before racing to their team member at the end of the track. On arrival they must take the outfit off and pass it to the next player, who puts the clothes on as quickly as possible before racing back to the next player.

- First team across the finishing line wins.

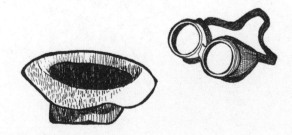

Household Horseshoes

What's the game?

The traditional horseshoe game found at country fairs across the country can also be turned into an indoor event when played with a toilet brush and holder. Great for inactive game-playing while nestled on the sofa.

What do I need to play it?

An unused toilet brush in its holder and anything shaped in a ring, such as a piece of rope tied in a circle, a bracelet or pastry cutter. You need three for each player, though if you're short you can pass them between you.

How many kids?

A minimum of two children, but no more than four. This loses its appeal if there's too much waiting around.

How do I play it?

- Maintain a comfortable position on the sofa and position the toilet brush at an achievable, though challenging, distance.

- Players take it in turns to score points by getting their 'ring thing' over the stick at the top of the toilet-brush holder.

Nine

Fun for
Car Journeys

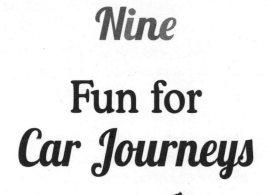

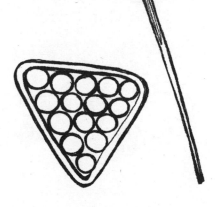

We've all been there: stuck in a car with a fidgeting, scrapping, crying pack of kids. It's a dead cert that during any journey of over an hour, interludes of pure hell will be endured.

Games, as any well-travelled parent will know, are the most valuable tools in these situations. As children can be known to demonstrate Lucifer-like traits at such times, it is recommended that you travel armed with a variety of entertainment delights, as well as some secret-weapon winners up your sleeve.

Make Your Own Fun

Car Scavenger Hunt

What's the game?

The much-loved game of Scavenger Hunt can be played on a car journey with ease. It'll keep your beloveds occupied in gazing out of the window for hours, leaving you to get on with the driving.

What do I need to play it?

Some pens and paper.

How many kids and what age?

This game works for a carful of kids of all ages.

How do I play it?

• You need to do a spot of preparatory work first by writing up a sheet for each child featuring a long list of animals, types of trees, colours of cars, road signs and so on. To prevent arguments, this works best if you give each child their own individual list without duplicating any of the items. If any child gets carsick, another child can read the list to them and tick off their 'spots'.

• The first one to spot all the items on their list is the winner.

Farm Wars

What's the game?

This one's meant for young kids and involves points being awarded for animals that are spotted along the way. It's best played on country roads, as the speed on a motorway can make it tricky to identify what's in each field.

What do I need to play it?

A car travelling on a relatively slow road.

How many kids and what age?

As many kids as you have in your car. This game is suitable for all ages.

How do I play it?

- Half the car looks out for cows and the other half is on sheep. You score one point for each field of cows or sheep that you pass. If you pass a cemetery you lose all your points. The game plays on until you reach your destination and whoever scores the most points wins.

- You can make up additional rules based on the type of journey you're making. So, if you're travelling through an urban area, you might award a point if you spot someone walking a dog, and if you can get that person to wave to you, you score five points.

Make a Smiley Friend

What's the game?

One of the beauties of motorway driving is that you can get your kids to engage in conversations with passengers in other cars. You've probably seen it before – kids waving frantically out of the back window, desperately trying to get your attention before collapsing in a heap of giggles. This game is a friendly version of that.

What do I need to play it?

Some smiling kids.

How many kids and what age?

A carful of kids of all ages.

How do I play it?

- Kids take it in turn to beam out of the car window at passengers (not drivers) in other cars. They have sixty seconds to make someone smile. They score a point for every smile they get.

- The child with the most smile points at the end of the game is the winner.

Number-Plate Bingo

What's the game?

This one is ideal for long motorway journeys, or if you have to endure the mundane hell of being stuck in a traffic jam.

What do I need to play it?

Some pens and paper.

How many kids and what age?

A carful of kids aged six and over. They need to be old enough to know the alphabet.

How do I play it?

- Prepare some bingo cards for each child by drawing up a nine-square grid and going through the alphabet and plotting random letters in each of the boxes. You might want to prepare a few cards if you're on a long journey.

- Distribute these to the kids along with a pen each, and then as you drive along randomly shout out the first letter on car number plates that you pass. The kids cross off the letter if it appears on their grid.

- The winner is the child who completes their bingo card first.

The Twisty Road Game

What's the game?

Some friends of mine called Chris and Esther developed this game to entertain their young children on long arduous journeys; it's ideal for kids who are refusing to doze off. You really need to be driving along windy country roads at night to get the full effect, as it involves trying to guess how many turns of the road you can clear without another car passing you by.

What do I need to play it?

Some wide-awake kids on windy country roads.

How many kids and what age?

As many as are in the car. As long as a child can count they can play.

How do I play it?

- Each player has to predict in turn how many bends in the road the car can go around without another vehicle passing in the opposite direction.

- A total number of bends for players to achieve is set at the start. Try fifty, but this can be adapted to a particular road's bendiness or busyness.

- The first person to go makes a prediction, for example: 'We'll get around six bends without a car passing'. If he or she is correct, they score six points. If a vehicle does pass by, that player loses six points (a minus-point situation may occur as the game plays on).

- Player two then makes their prediction and so on. The first to fifty points wins and the loser is on carwash duty.

The Word Association Game

What's the game?

For those of you who grew up in the 1980s, this game is very similar to one played regularly on Timmy Mallett's Saturday-morning show *Wacaday*. I used to love that show and when a friend of mine recently announced she'd been a guest on 'Bonk and Boob', I felt a deep pang of jealousy.

This simple game involves players having to quickly come up with words that are associated with the one that was mentioned before. It's a great mind exercise for the kids and the random associations they come up with can prove pretty entertaining for adults too. Another game that's great to roll out wherever you are.

What do I need to play it?

Some fast-thinking kids.

How many kids and what age?

Ideal for two or a carful of kids aged six and upwards.

How do I play it?

- Arrange the kids in order so that they know whose turn it is next. Start by giving the first person a word, and they must come up with a word associated with it. For example, if the word given was 'rug', the next child might say 'vacuum' or 'carpet', and the next child might say 'floor' or 'skirting board'.

- If a child pauses for too long or says a word that is totally unrelated to the one before, that child is out.

- The game keeps playing around and around until one child is left in who is declared the winner.

Fizz Buzz

What's the game?

You might think on first glance that this one should be confined to maths class, but it's great fun to play and only requires a very basic grasp of times tables.

What do I need to play it?

Nothing.

How many kids and what age?

You could play it with two of you, but it's great to play with a carful. Kids really need to be aged nine and upwards or at least have a solid grasp of numbers.

How do I play it?

- Arrange the kids in order so that they know whose turn it is next. They take it in turns to count, so the first player would say 'one', the next would say 'two' and so on.

- When a player gets to a number that is divisible by three they must say 'Fizz', and when they reach one that's divisible by five they must say 'Buzz'. If they reach one that is divisible by both, they must say 'Fizz Buzz'.

- Every player gets five points to start with and then loses one each time they get a response wrong. When they have no points left, they're out.

- The game keeps playing around and around until one child is left in who is declared the winner.

Animal, Vegetable, Mineral

What's the game?

I've got a misty memory of playing this as a child, though we always called it Twenty Questions from what I can remember. This Victorian parlour game involves trying to guess what the other person is thinking of by asking no more than twenty 'yes' or 'no' questions to determine what it might be. Its adult entertainment value is fairly limited, but it will engage kids for hours on long dull car journeys.

What do I need to play it?

Nothing.

How many kids and what age?

Works best in smaller groups of kids aged five and upwards.

How do I play it?

- Take it in turns to play. The first child thinks of something and the rest of the players try to guess what it is, gathering clues by asking twenty questions that can only be answered 'yes' or 'no'.

- The first question is 'Is it an animal?', and then if the answer's no, the next person asks 'Is it a mineral?', and finally, if it's still a no, 'Is it a vegetable?' Subsequent questions might be 'Does it have wings?' or 'Is it edible?', for example. Wrong guesses count as a question.

- Once the right answer is guessed, it's the next child's turn to think of something. If no one has guessed correctly after twenty questions, the child has won a point or another go.

Cheesy-Puff Sculptures

What's the game?

My packed lunches were wholewheat drudgery when I was a child. I think my mum must have been going through a yoghurt-weaving hippie stage at the time, as the most exciting thing to ever appear in my lunchbox was a mini packet of raisins as a treat.

On Sundays after church I got my twenty-five-pence pocket money, which funded a sugar rush served up via the local corner shop. As I also wanted to get a copy of the *Beano*, it often meant a tough decision between entertainment or tasty titbits. By chance, I discovered that cheesy puffs provided both for the price of one. These cheesy snacks soon became my nibble of choice when I realised the fun that could be had from creating DayGlo orange sculptures.

What do I need to play it?

A packet of cheesy puffs per child. It only works with puffed-style crisps.

How many kids and what age?

As many as want to play. The younger they are, the more mess they're likely to make of your upholstery.

How do I play it?

- The object of the game is to craft the most creative and impressive sculpture out of cheesy puffs.
- To sculpt using cheesy puffs, simply bite the top of one of them off, lick it and stick another one on top. A bit of pressure will ensure a durable piece of craftsmanship.
- The best sculpture wins.

A to Z

What's the game?

This is another one to roll out on a long and tedious journey. At first you'll be delighted by its ability to engage kids for hours and it will be played again and again, before it drives you slowly around the bend. It involves listing the A to Z of items in a specific category, from types of chairs to breeds of dog – trust me, the list is truly endless.

What do I need to play it?

Fast-thinking brains, ones that ideally contain a full working knowledge of the *Encyclopaedia Britannica*.

How many kids and what age?

As many as are in the car. As long as they have a basic grasp of spelling, they'll be able to play.

How do I play it?

- Split into two teams. One team nominates a category for the opposing team, who must list items in that category from A to Z. If the chosen category was cars, you might start with Aston Martin, followed by a BMW and so on.

- Each go runs until the team can't think of an item that corresponds to the next letter. Points are awarded for the number of items they correctly come up with.

- Once their points are counted up, that team now nominates a category for the other team, who must also list items in that category from A to Z. The game plays on in the same way until either the first team to reach 100 points wins or until you reach your destination.

- This one's great for older kids, but just make sure your team split ensures any youngsters are partnered with an adult.

Taboo

What's the game?

The classic game of Taboo consists of players taking it in turns to explain a word without saying the word itself or any part of it.

What do I need to play it?

Pens, paper and a stopwatch.

How many kids and what age?

Ideal for two or a carful of kids aged nine and upwards.

How do I play it?

- Get yourself prepared by writing out a list of words (I'd go for about ten per player) and cut them up into slips of paper and pop them in a hat.

- Split the players into teams.

- A player from the first team starts by pulling a slip of paper out of the hat and describing the word. If, for example, the word was 'bench', the player might say, 'Brown wooden thing for people to sit on that you often find in parks.'

- The aim is to get through as many words as possible in one minute. Once the minute is up, players count up the number of words they managed to describe and play moves on to the next team.

- You can pass if you get stuck on a word, but each player is only allowed to do this once during their go.

- The game continues until everyone on each of the teams has had a go describing. The team with the highest score wins.

Make Your Own Fun

Better Letter

What's the game?

This is another winner for confined spaces, with the added advantage of working for adults as well as kids. Children need to be old enough to have a strong vocabulary and a good grasp of spelling. The game involves slowly building a word letter by letter, with players trying not to be the person who adds the last letter.

What do I need to play it?

Nothing.

How many kids and what age?

A carful of kids who are good at spelling and have a strong vocabulary.

How do I play it?

- The aim of the game is to create a word by taking it in turns to add the next letter. Whoever is obliged to add the final letter loses the game.

- So for example, if the first four players in turn chose the letters 'C', 'R', 'E' and 'A', subsequent players could then choose to build on it so that it becomes 'creativity', 'creation' or 'creatures', depending on which word ensures they won't be left with the last letter when it comes back around to their turn.

- Plurals and past tenses are of course allowed.

Car Snooker

What's the game?

This game involves the same point system as for snooker, but instead of potting balls, you have to spot cars.

What do I need to play it?

You need to be travelling on a road with a fair amount of traffic; it doesn't work as well on quiet country lanes. It's also a good idea to have a pad and pen to keep track of scores and a stopwatch of some sort to time each round.

How many kids and what age?

A carful of kids aged six and over.

How do I play it?

- Each player has two minutes, timed by the grown-up passenger in the front.

- If, for example, a player spots a red car when it's their go, they score one point. The highest scoring car is a black one, which will give you seven points. For those not familiar with the game of snooker, the points awarded for each colour are shown below:

  - A red car = 1 point.
  - A yellow car = 2 points.
  - A green car = 3 points.
  - A brown car or any lorry = 4 points.
  - A blue car = 5 points.
  - A pink car = 6 points.
  - A black car = 7 points.

- The player with the highest score at the end of the journey wins.

Alphabet Signs

What's the game?

This is great for young kids who are learning to read and write. It involves working your way through the alphabet using the first letters of road signs.

What do I need to play it?

A road with lots of easily readable signs. Motorways and well-signposted cities are perfect; you might struggle to play it on country lanes.

How many kids and what age?

All those in the car. Great for youngsters who are learning to read and write.

How do I play it?

- The object is to spot a road sign beginning with the next sequential letter in the alphabet.

- So for example, someone might spot a sign to 'Andover' to begin with, and the next spot might be 'Brick Lane'. (Clearly this is hypothetical!) Each correct spot scores a point and the game plays on until the full alphabet is completed. The child with the most points wins.

Make Your Own Fun

Silly Sentences

What's the game?

This game is basically Consequences Lite and is great for kids of all ages who've learnt how to talk. The younger the child, the more entertaining it should end up being, but this is another one that also works for adults.

What do I need to play it?

Nothing.

How many kids and what age?

A carful of kids who are of talking age.

How do I play it?

- In this game, players make up coherent sentences by taking it in turns to contribute a word, for example: 'Sarah' 'hated' 'salami'. . .

- Kids love to drag this one out to create stupidly daft and long sentences.

- Ideally you want the game to play with a bit of pace. Once they start getting good at it, get them to move on to a mini story.

Ten

How to Put On the Best *Children's Party Ever*

Kids' parties were always the same
when I was a child, from the children arriving
with their scrubbed faces and favourite frocks to
the obligatory squished slice of birthday cake on
departure wrapped in a couple of greasy sheets
of kitchen roll. The same could also be said of the
games that always took place. Proceedings were
generally kicked off with Pass the Parcel, reaching a
peak with Musical Chairs and ending with a game
of Sleeping Lions, in a vague attempt to get the kids
down off their sugar-crazed highs before
being carted off home.

There's nothing wrong with this
traditional approach, but as kids only get one
chance at being a kid, I think we owe it to them
to make their birthday experiences as
fun-packed as possible.

When it comes to the entertainment,
the following chapter ensures you'll have a stack
of ammunition worthy of the Terminator. It's packed
full of novel ideas to keep you in the driving
seat at all times.

Helpful Hints

Here are a few guidelines to help you put on the best children's party ever:

1. If your child wants to theme their birthday party, let them. Their subject choice may not be aesthetically to your liking, or you might struggle to find or make a pterodactyl costume, but after all it's their day and this is their chance to get all their friends and family to play their favourite games. You don't have to theme everything; a spot of creative renaming is all you need. Chocolate cornflake cakes can make great caveman rocks and Musical Statues can be turned into a game of Musical Dinosaur Shapes.

2. Planning is something that comes more naturally to some people than others. When faced with a teeming beaming room of kids looking expectantly to you to be entertained, planning becomes a necessity. Work out how much time you have and calculate how many games you think you'll need to fill the slot, and then double it. You'll be surprised how quickly they'll get through them, and once you've got them worked into a frenzy, if you run out of ways to hold their attention anarchy will undoubtedly ensue.

3. Announce every game and activity with eye-popping enthusiasm. They will cheer with delight if you present each one as the most exciting thing to happen since finding Rudolf had eaten the carrots left out for him on Christmas Eve. My sisters and I recently had the pleasure of organising the entertainment at our cousin Leon's birthday party. The kids had whipped themselves into such a frenzy that we only had to bound along with the same air-punching delight and we had them squealing with glee at every suggestion.

4. You should also never show you're scared. Children have the same admirable power of perception as animals and they can sniff out a note of fear in a nanosecond. Delivery and conduct must ooze confidence throughout.

5. Finally, bribery works. From rewarding well-earned wins to encouraging game participation, a stash of chewy delights is the magic dust to ensure proceedings go swimmingly. Sadly, not every child is blessed with a taste for pulses and greens, so you'll probably need something less wholesome than a carrot stick to encourage them to do your bidding.

Fancy-Dress Pass the Parcel

What's the game?

Same principle as for Pass the Parcel, but this time when the music stops, the player holding the parcel has to take an item of clothing out of a bag and put it on.

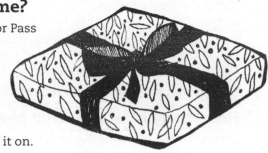

What do I need to play it?

Get a carrier bag and fill it with lots of different items of clothing, the funnier the better. Think stupid wigs or kids dressed in adults' clothes and you'll get the idea. You'll also need a stereo to play some music to accompany the passing.

How many kids and what age?

Great for large groups of children aged five and upwards.

How do I play it?

- Collect your dressing-up clothes together and put them in a bag.
- Next, get all the children to sit in a circle.
- When the music starts, the children start to pass the parcel around, and when the music stops they have to reach into the bag, pull out an item and put it on.
- The music then starts again and the game continues.
- The child who puts the last item on is the winner.

Corners

What's the game?

This game's a great one to start off the party entertainment. It's easy to explain and kids grasp it quickly.

What do I need to play it?

A room with four corners and something for a blindfold.

How many kids and what age?

Lots and lots – the more the better, as ten is the minimum you can really play with. Children ideally need to be seven and above to fully understand it.

How do I play it?

- Choose a room with four corners and number them one to four, making sure all the kids know which corner has been given which number.

- Choose which child is going to be 'it' first and blindfold them.

- The rest of the children then split up randomly and run to one of the four corners of the room.

- The blindfolded child then shouts out a number and all the children in that corner are out.

- The kids then break up again and run to another corner in the room, and so the game plays on until the last child or children in the game are the winners. It's then one of their turns to be blindfolded next.

Knights, Horses and Cavaliers

What's the game?

This is a wonderful alternative to Musical Statues and bang on the money for kids who find the classic games a little too childish.

What do I need to play it?

Nothing.

How many kids and what age?

Ideally an equal pairing of boys and girls in the group. Works best for kids aged eight upwards. Also good for young teens if you can coax them out of their adolescent stroppiness.

How do I play it?

- Get your young friends to pair up, ideally with someone from the opposite sex.

- When the music's on, the pairs must prance and dance around at will. When the music stops, the facilitator shouts either 'Knight', 'Horse' or 'Cavalier'.

- 'Knight' means the male has to give his partner a piggyback, 'Horse' means the male has to give their partner a horse ride by getting on all fours, and 'Cavalier' means the male has to get down on one knee and the female sits on the uppermost knee.

- The last couple to execute the manoeuvre is out. The game plays on until the last remaining couple is announced the winner.

Musical Chairs

What's the game?

Musical Chairs is a children's party classic. For those not familiar with the game, it involves dancing around chairs and dashing to sit down when the music stops.

What do I need to play it?

A stereo or something to make the music. Chairs.

How many kids?

Brilliant for a huge group, but it will obviously depend on how many chairs you've got.

How do I play it?

- First of all, get yourself set up by lining up two rows of chairs back to back down the middle of the room. You need a big playing space, so clear other furniture out of the way. You also need to ensure that there are enough chairs for everyone playing the game minus one. If there are just a few children playing, you could use your tea table as the set-up.

- Put the music on and get everyone to dance around the chairs. To make sure there's no aggressive chair coveting, people need to keep moving around as they dance.

- At a point when people least expect it, turn the music off and players must dash to a chair and sit down on it. The last person to do this is out. No sitting on laps is allowed.

- Before putting the music back on, move another chair out of the field of play.

- The game continues in the same way until there's one chair and two people left. The first to sit down wins.

Musical Statues

What's the game?

This one's simple for kids to grasp and only requires a stereo to play. It's ideal for getting the kids razzed up and excited before kicking off an afternoon of game playing.

What do I need to play it?

A stereo or something to make the music. You can strum or pluck a few ditties yourself if you have the ability and inclination.

How many kids and what age?

At least eight to make it a decent game and they need to be old enough to stand up, dance and stop. I'd say great for those aged four and over.

How do I play it?

- Get your gang to spread out in front of you and put the music on.
- The children must then dance about.
- You turn the music off at random intervals, at which point the kids must freeze.
- The last child (or children) to freeze is out and must sit on the floor at the side. Anyone else who moves at all while the music's off is also out.
- If you've got a big group, keep an eye out for those cunning kids who slip around the sides and out of your view. Another tactic is to move very slightly and slowly to the music so that it's easier to stay stock still when commanded.
- The winner is of course the last child standing.
- The best bit about the game when I was a child was when the adults would walk around us mid-freeze, tickling us and pulling faces to try to make us laugh.

218

Musical Bumps

What's the game?

This is a great variation on Musical Statues in which the kids must sit down when the music stops. It's a good alternative when you're playing in large groups, as it's easier to spot the last child to sit down rather than the last one moving.

What do I need to play it?

A room or contained area and some music.

How many kids and what age?

Great for large groups aged four and over. I'd say you probably need a minimum of eight players to make it go on for any length of time.

How do I play it?

- Put on some music and get your gang of kids to dance about.
- When they least expect it, turn off the music and all the kids must quickly sit on the floor.
- Last one to sit down is out and must go and sit quietly at the side. Last one left in is the winner.

Musical Human Chairs

What's the game?

Musical Human Chairs is a great alternative to the original Musical Chairs when you don't have a stash of chairs to hand. It's also a good game to play with a group of mixed ages, or if children and adults are both involved. In this version, chairs are replaced by humans going down on their hands and knees to create a chair shape.

What do I need to play it?

Something to make the music.

How many kids and what age?

As before, at least eight to make it a decent game, and they need to be old enough to stand up, dance and stop. I'd say this is great for those aged four and over. If the parents are around, this game works really well if the parents partner with their kids.

How do I play it?

- Get everyone to pair up and decide who's the chair and who's the human.

- Once everyone's fully aware of their chair or human status, the game proceeds as with a standard game of Musical Chairs, but this time when the music stops, the chairs get on their hands and knees and the humans sit on top. The last pair to get into position are out.

- The last pair in wins.

Make Your Own Fun

The Chocolate-Honeycomb-Ball Game

What's the game?

This was a regular feature at my childhood birthday parties. It involves sucking a chocolate honeycomb ball onto a straw and racing to see who can get the most chocolate honeycomb balls into their pot.

What do I need to play it?

A large bag of chocolate honeycomb balls, a bowl and a timer. Each player also needs a straw and a cup.

How many kids and what age?

However many are around. It works best for children aged eight and over.

How do I play it?

- Empty the chocolate honeycomb balls into the bowl and place it in the middle of the table. Each player sits around the bowl with a straw and cup in hand.

- Children are each given thirty seconds to suck chocolate honeycomb balls onto the end of their straw and transport them from the bowl in the middle to the cup in their hand.

- Once everyone's had their go, the child with the most chocolate honeycomb balls in their cup wins.

Islands

What's the game?

This is another great alternative to Musical Chairs if you don't have enough chairs to play with. The same rules apply, but you just use newspapers instead.

What do I need to play it?

An old newspaper and some music.

How many kids and what age?

A minimum of six to make it a decent-length game. This one's ideal for kids aged five and over.

How do I play it?

- Lay out sheets of newspaper at a reasonable distance apart from each other to create 'islands' on the floor or grass. You need to lay out enough sheets so that there's one less than the number of children playing.

- Put on some music and get the children to skip and dance around the sheets. When the music stops, the children have to leap onto an island. The child with no island to stand on is out.

- You then remove one of the sheets and play on until one child is left in and is declared the winner.

Toilet-Paper Mummies

What's the game?

I'm not quite sure what the appeal is, but this is one of my favourites. It sounds ridiculous when described, but bear with me and give it a go. It's another one that's great for adults and kids. To save wasting valuable resources, make sure you get the kids to wind the toilet roll back up for future use. But be warned: you are left with an inelegant pile of unhygienic bottom-wiping material. Might be best saved for other mopping-up uses.

What do I need to play it?

Toilet rolls: one for each team.

How many kids and what age?

As many teams as you like, though ideally no more than three in each team. Great for kids of all ages.

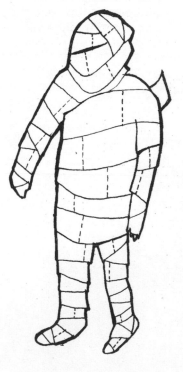

How do I play it?

- Split players into teams of three and give each team a toilet roll.

- Decide who's going to be the Egyptian mummy and stand them in the middle between the other two players. The two players then wrap the third in the toilet roll by winding it around them so that they look like an Egyptian mummy. If the toilet roll breaks, they must tuck in the broken end and carry on.

- The winning team is the one who makes the best mummy in two minutes.

- Once done, get the kids to carefully wind the paper back onto the toilet roll.

Piñata

What's the game?

Piñata is a traditional Mexican game that forms the
highlight of kids' parties in Mexico and across the States.
It's best played outdoors as you need something like a tree
to hang your piñata from and enough room to swing the
stick. You can buy piñatas from toyshops or online, but I've
included instructions on how you can make your own. It
requires a bit of effort a few days in advance, but this in
itself is half the fun and great for getting kids involved.

What do I need to play it?

Five cups of water, quarter of a cup of plain flour, a large
balloon, some string, a pile of old newspapers, plain white
paper, paint, a paintbrush, a serrated knife, masking tape
and lots of small sweets, toys and shredded paper to fill your
piñata with once finished. You also need some bits and pieces
from your recycling box to create your piñata's features.

How many kids and what age?

Great for kids of all ages and ideal for a big group at a child's
party.

How to make the piñata

- To make the papier-mâché: mix a small amount of water
  with the flour in a pan to create a smooth paste and
  slowly add the rest of the water, before gently boiling
  for two to three minutes. The paste should just start to
  thicken; don't cook it for any longer than this, as it will
  stop it being sticky.

- Next, tear up some newspaper to make strips about ten
  centimetres long and two centimetres wide. Take each
  strip, smear it with the cooled flour glue and lay the strips
  over the blown-up balloon until it is completely covered in
  a thick layer of papier-mâché. After the first layer, attach a

long piece of string to the top of the balloon by pasting more strips of paper over one end of the string to hold it firmly in place, and then continue covering the whole balloon with a second layer of strips. Continue adding papier-mâché until there are three thick layers covering the balloon. To make things easier for you when you come to painting the balloon later, make the last layer out of plain paper, which is easier to paint. Now leave it somewhere safe to dry.

- Once dried, use a serrated knife to cut out a flap and then pop the balloon and remove it. Fill the papier-mâché balloon-shaped shell with sweets, small toys and shredded coloured paper. Tape the flap shut using masking tape so you can still paint over the top.

- Next is the fun bit. You need to decide what animal you want to make your piñata into and then cut out shapes from your spare bits of recycling cardboard to create ears, a nose and eyes. We used a toilet roll to create a pig's ears and nose and then cut out a curly piece of card for the pig's tail.

- Then get your paints out and paint your piñata the colour of your choosing and leave it to dry somewhere safe.

- Finally, hang it up from the tree with the string.

How do I play it?

- When you're ready to play, gather all the children around the piñata. Each child takes it in turn to be blindfolded and spun around and then with stick in hand they have to try to walk towards the hanging piñata and take a swipe at it to knock it down or knock a hole in it to get the sweets and toys inside.

- Each child has two swipes. If a child is under three, don't worry about the blindfold; just let them have their two swipes without it. Also, let younger kids go first so the older ones don't knock the piñata down early on.

- The winner is the one who knocks a hole in the piñata or knocks it out of the tree.

Shark Attack!

What's the game?

This game involves splitting your group into sharks and fish who chase each other around the harbour walls. Be prepared for a screaming shoal of kids.

What do I need to play it?

A pile of clothes or bags to mark out the harbour walls.

How many kids and what age?

At least twelve kids aged seven and over.

How do I play it?

- Set up your harbour walls by laying out the bags and coats in a five-metre-long line, leaving an opening of about two metres marking the harbour entrance.

- Get the kids to stand in a line and go along the line giving them each the name of a different type of fish, e.g. plaice, cod, mackerel and so on, and then every fourth person is a shark. It might be worth running through their names a couple of times to make sure they know who they are.

- Once this is established, you need to manoeuvre everyone to get all the fish on one side of the wall and the sharks on the other.

- One by one, shout out the different fish names and as each name is called that fish must leave the harbour. Leave the sharks in the harbour.
- Once they're all out, encourage them to swim about and around each other.
- When they're least expecting it, you shout 'Shark attack!' and the sharks leap over the walls and into action to try to catch a fish. Meanwhile, the fish must try to run back into the harbour through the entrance. Once through the harbour entrance the fish are then safe.
- Any fish caught by the shark are then out and must go and sit at the side.
- The game plays on until there's only one fish left who's declared the winner.
- Be prepared for lots of squealing.

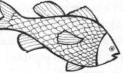

Stepping Stones

What's the game?

This is a race across the room in which players are only allowed to step on pieces of newspaper that they lay out in front of them.

What do I need to play it?

Two sheets of newspaper per player.

How many kids and what age?

A good crowd to make it a race. It really depends on how much room you have available to play the game. This one's suitable for children aged six and upwards.

How do I play it?

- Get the kids to line up at a designated starting point with their sheets of paper in hand.

- On the word 'Go!', they have to race to the finishing line but they are only allowed to tread on the sheets of paper that they lay out in front of them. As they step with both feet onto the first sheet they need to lay out their second sheet, and so they move forwards by turning around to pick up the sheet behind them and moving it to the front for them to step on, and so on.

- To introduce an element of pretend danger, you could announce that the carpet is shark-infested – make sure you stick to the stepping stones!

- The first to the finishing line wins.

Shoe Tag

What's the game?

A variation on the classic game of Tag. This one gives the kids two lives and has the added attraction of having their shoes stuffed down their trousers or skirts to keep them absorbed that little bit longer.

What do I need to play it?

Children with shoes that will fit down the backs of their trousers or skirts. If the girls are wearing dresses, you'll need something that can be used to make belts.

How many kids and what age?

A big rambling crowd of kids aged six and above.

How do I play it?

- Get the kids to put their shoes either down the backs of their trousers or skirts or tuck them securely underneath a belt. You need to ensure that each child has a reasonable amount of shoe sticking out of the top so that the other kids can grab it.

- Choose who's 'it' and whoever it is has to chase after the other kids and try to pull a shoe out of the back of their trousers, skirt or belt.

- Once a shoe is grabbed, these are then put at the side. A player becomes 'it' when both their shoes have been taken.

Stalkers

What's the game?

This is a game that seemed synonymous with children's parties in the 1980s. I remember playing it at Girl Guides before I got asked to leave for bad behaviour.

What do I need to play it?

A chair, a blindfold and a set of keys.

How many kids and what age?

A minimum of three to make it fun. It works best with kids aged seven and over.

How do I play it?

- Decide which child is going first and blindfold them, then sit them on the chair with a set of keys underneath the chair.

- The other children have to try and sneak up one by one without being 'sensed' and snatch the keys from under the chair.

- The child on the chair has to sense where they are by pointing in the direction he or she thinks the stalking child is coming from.

- If they get it right, the child who was busted is next in the chair.

Pin the Kiss on the Poster

What's the game?

This is a great alternative to
Pin the Tail on the Donkey
and very amusing for
everyone to watch.

What do I need to play it?

Some full-fat Marilyn Monroe
red lipstick and a poster or picture
from a magazine of your selected idol.

How many kids and what age?

Any more than six and the game loses its momentum.
Smaller groups are much better. This one's great for younger
kids as it's easy for them to grasp. It works for anyone aged
four and upwards.

How do I play it?

- First of all, hang the picture of the kids' idol at kissing
  height for the players.

- Next, children take it in turns to layer up with a good
  coating of lipstick and then put the blindfold on.

- When ready, the child is spun around several times to
  create a sense of disorientation and then gently propelled
  towards the poster.

- The object of the game is for the child to attempt to kiss
  the idol's lips. Every time a kiss is planted, you write the
  child's name near it so you know whose kiss it is.

- The planter of the closest kiss wins.

Dunking Relay

What's the game?

This was the most talked-about party game of the year when my friend Deborah played it at her birthday party when I was younger. Kids absolutely adore it as they are given permission to get filthy dirty and covered in flour.

What do I need to play it?

Two washing-up bowls or buckets, six apples, two smaller bowls of flour (a ceramic mixing bowl is perfect; fill it about a quarter full) and some sweets in wrappers. It's also good to have a bowl of warm water, flannels and towels to wash and dry each child's face after they've completed the challenge.

How many kids and what age?

Great for large groups of kids aged five and over.

How do I play it?

- This is a novel version of a relay race, where kids have to race to two different bowls to complete different activities before returning to their team.

- First of all, divide the group into two teams.

- Lay out a starting line. Half-fill the two washing-up bowls or buckets with water and float three apples in each. Position the buckets about a metre after the line. Then position the two bowls of flour a metre after the buckets and put some wrapped sweets in each, making sure there's at least one for each member of the team.

- Get the teams lined up behind the starting line and on the word 'Go!' the first member of each team races to their bucket and has to dunk their head and bite an apple out of the water before placing it back into the bucket. Once that's achieved, they then race to the next bowl and have to dunk their wet face in the bowl of flour to grab a sweet before racing back to their team, at which point the next person sets off.

- The first team to complete the course wins.

British Bulldog

What's the game?

I was never quite sure what the trigger was, but every so often a rumour went around our school that everyone was going to play British Bulldog. The ripples of anticipation that went through each and every classroom were palpable and by the time the bell rang for lunch the entire school would come tumbling down the steps onto the tarmac and form themselves into one gargantuan heap that stood facing a single player.

The potential hairiness of this game always had the teachers hovering nervously on the periphery, muttering into their fingers about whether they should intervene. Keep an eye on any notoriously boisterous kids to ensure they don't get carried away in the excitement of it all.

What do I need to play it?

A big gang of kids and a large area to play in. It's also good to somehow mark out the play area with chalk if you're playing on tarmac. Alternatively, bags do the job just as well.

How many kids and what age?

Ideal for ages nine and upwards. You need at least eight kids to make it last a decent amount of time.

How do I play it?

- Mark out two lines, behind which are the safety areas for players to race to.

- Choose who's going to be your Bulldog and position them in the middle, and get the rest of the kids to stand at one end of the play area facing them.

- When the Bulldog shouts 'Go!', all the children charge towards him or her. As the players are racing to the other side of the play area, the Bulldog has to tag as many players as possible.

- Once tagged, the caught player then joins the Bulldog to try to catch the others.

- The same process plays out again with the children racing from opposite sides of the play area, until there's one person left who is declared the winner who then becomes the Bulldog in the next game.

Sleeping Lions

What's the game?

It took me some time to figure out why Sleeping Lions was always the last game on any birthday-party agenda, but I was never the smartest kid on the block. For those who don't know it, it's the perfect way to calm a gaggle of razzed-up, sugar-fuelled kids.

What do I need to play it?

Some children who need to calm down.

How many kids?

As many or as few as you have.

How do I play it?

- Explain to the children that you're going to play a game of Sleeping Lions and that it involves lying on the floor and being as quiet and as still as is possible.

- If a child moves, they are out and must sit quietly at the side of the room.

- If it's been a particularly energetic day, you might be lucky enough to have a few children who drift gently off to sleep.

Make Your Own Fun

Acknowledgements

Special thanks to my mum for
being such a superstar, and for all
her ideas and support in making
this book come together.
Special thanks also to my godson
Samson Harding for his intellectual
and often challenging contributions
to the book.

List of Games

Make Your Own Fun

List of Games